ACTS OF GALLANTRY

VOLUME THREE

BEING

A DETAILED ACCOUNT OF DEEDS OF BRAVERY
IN SAVING LIFE, 1951 - 2000

FOR WHICH THE ROYAL HUMANE SOCIETY
AWARDED
THE SILVER MEDAL
THE POLICE MEDAL
& THE STANHOPE GOLD MEDAL

accompanied by

CITATIONS FOR ALL BRONZE MEDALS
WITH CLASPS, 1869 - 2000

Compiled by

WILLIAM H. FEVYER & CRAIG P. BARCLAY

The Naval & Military Press, 2002

ACTS OF GALLANTRY
VOLUME THREE
1951 TO 2000

Also by W.H. Fevyer
The George Medal 1940 - 1945
The Distinguished Service Medal 1939 - 1946
The Distinguished Service Medal 1914 - 1920
The Distinguished Service Cross 1901 - 1938
Acts of Gallantry Volume 2, 1871-1950

Also by C.P. Barclay
The Medals of the Royal Humane Society

First Published 2002 by
The Naval and Military Press

© W.H. Fevyer 2001
© C.P. Barclay 2001
© Royal Humane Society 2001

All rights reserved. No part of this publication may be reproduced, stored in a retrieval system or transmitted in any form by any means, electrical, mechanical or otherwise without first seeking the written permission of the copyright holders.

Printed in
Great Britain
By
The Naval and Military Press

FOREWORD

In the Foreword to the second Volume of *Acts of Gallantry* (1871-1950) my predecessor, Major A.J. (Dick) Dickinson, pointed out that Lambton J.H. Young, who wrote the first of these compilations of awards, was an expert due to being Secretary of the Royal Humane Society for twenty years. What Dick failed to say was that he himself had held the appointment for seventeen years and was therefore an expert himself. I have not yet completed six years so I am still a beginner and rely very heavily on the knowledge and experience of the two compilers of this third Volume.

I have never met Bill Fevyer but I have spoken to him on the telephone many times, seeking his advice. Craig Barclay, who has taken over from Bill as the Secretary of the Life Saving Awards Research Society, has been a regular visitor to our offices while researching either for this book or for his definitive work on the medals of the Royal Humane Society. Craig has taken on the mantle of 'guru' to historical matters and each of them is the epitome of a researcher: tenacious, patient, accurate and benign!

Volume III joins its forerunners on an equal footing and I only hope that we have such talent available when Volume IV is required.

Major General C. Tyler CB MA
Brettenham House, 2001

INTRODUCTION

The majority of the details reproduced in this volume have been taken from the records of the Royal Humane Society. Wherever possible, the date of the incident and the occupation of the recipient have been included. We are greatly indebted to the Secretary of the Society, Major General Christopher Tyler CB, and his staff for all their help and encouragement.

In researching the recipients of Stanhope Gold Medals, the authors were also fortunate to have been provided with invaluable assistance by the representatives of a number of associated Societies. In particular we would like to thank Sue Cutler of the Royal Humane Society of Australasia; J.F. Bertram and Nina Smith of the Royal Humane Society of New South Wales; E. Gordon Williams of the Liverpool Shipwreck and Humane Society; and John Mills of the Royal Humane Society of New Zealand. Our thanks are also due to Jack Boddington for additional information and to Kim Oldfield for formatting much of the original typescript.

When reading through the citations reproduced between these covers, it is impossible not to be moved by the courage of the rescuers whose deeds are recorded. Whilst the circumstances surrounding many of the incidents described would have been unimaginable to the eighteenth-century founders of the Society, they would surely have recognised and approved of the humane instincts of all those who have risked their lives to save others.

Bill Fevyer
Craig Barclay
September 2001

This Book is dedicated
to the memory of

Marjory Robson,

without whose help, support and enthusiasm
it could never have been written.

CONTENTS

STANHOPE GOLD MEDALS 1951-2000	**page 1**
POLICE MEDAL 2000	**page 31**
SILVER MEDALS 1951-2000	**page 35**
BRONZE MEDALS WITH CLASPS	**page 57**
INDEX TO STANHOPE MEDALS	**page 115**
INDEX TO POLICE MEDALS	**page 116**
INDEX TO SILVER MEDALS	**page 117**
INDEX TO BRONZE MEDALS WITH CLASPS	**page 118**
INDEX TO ADDITIONAL BRONZE MEDALS	**page 121**
INDEX TO RHS TESTIMONIALS	**page 122**
INDEX TO COMMONWEALTH & OTHER AWARDS	**page 123**

R.H.S. STANHOPE GOLD MEDALS

1951 to 2000

The Royal Humane Society
Stanhope Medal

The highest honour bestowed by the Royal Humane Society is the Stanhope Medal. This is given annually for the most gallant rescue to have been rewarded by the Society or, since 1962, by the Liverpool Shipwreck and Humane Society, or the Humane Societies of Australasia, Canada, New Zealand and New South Wales[1].

The Stanhope Medal was founded in 1873, in memory of Chandos Scudamore Scudamore Stanhope, an aristocratic naval recipient of the Society's silver medal who died of smallpox in Malta in 1871 at the age of 48[2]. The original funding for the medal was provided by the 'Stanhope Memorial Fund', whose Treasurer, A. Jones RN, offered the Royal Humane Society the funds necessary to award 'Annually a Gold Medal', to be called the 'Stanhope Medal'. The Committee of the Society resolved to accept this generous offer, agreeing[3]:

> *That the thanks of the Committee be transmitted through Mr Jones to the Committee of the Stanhope Memorial for their offer to the Society of the sum of £400 in trust, the interest of which shall be expended in giving a Gold medal annually to the case exhibiting the greatest gallantry during the year.*

The medal, which may be issued with either a 'successful' or 'unsuccessful' reverse according to circumstances, is identical in appearance to the Society's bronze and silver awards, other than insofar as it is struck in 9-carat gold. Prior to about 1936 however, the Stanhope Medal was suspended from a distinctive plaque-shaped bar, embossed with the date of award and the words STANHOPE MEDAL, whilst the adoption of nine as opposed to 18-carat gold did not occur until 1942[4]. In 2000, modified obverse and reverse designs by Avril Vaughan were adopted for use on the Society's medals.

---

[1] A.J. Dickinson, 'A System of Awards', *Life Saving Awards Research Society Journal* 5, 1989, pp. 14-15.

[2] E. A. J. van Engeland, 'Chandos Scudamore Scudamore Stanhope - A Biography', *Life Saving Awards Research Society Journal* 27, 1996, pp. 52-53.

[3] RHS Committee Minutes, 18 Feb. 1873.

[4] RHS Committee Minutes, 10 March 1942.

Williams, John, (55) Mine Captain　　　　　　　　　　　　　　　　　　　　　　　　　　　　　　　　Case 62338

Stanhope Gold Medal 1951

At 8 am on 31st October, 1950, at No 3 level of the Konongo Gold Mine, Gold Coast, West Africa, Briama Cardoe, an African citizen, was sent to pull stone from old chutes to infill chutes emptied from another level when a big stone came from the chute and overbalanced him. He fell into the cavity below and rock began to slide and fall burying him. Mr Williams and the other two salvors went down to the level, which is 455 feet below ground to try and get Mr Cardoe out, but the loose stones again started to move, endangering all four, Mr Williams promptly made a barrier of his body in an attempt to stop the flow. The effort was partly successful but not before Mr Cardoe was completely covered. Mr Williams and his helpers worked feverishly to uncover the victim's head and shoulders. This they did and were clearing him fully when the loose stones again began to run, covering Mr Cardoe. A rope and ladder were lowered to the rescuers enabling them to cut into the sides of the chute on the level of the victim's legs. This done they had to remove the stones from around the victim piece by piece while Mr Williams, by a great feat of strength and endurance, held back the loose stones by making a barrier of his body. Due to the efforts of the rescuers, especially Mr Williams, and complete disregard of personal safety, Mr Cardoe was rescued with no other injuries than a cut leg and cut forehead after having been trapped for 5 hours. Mr Shiels, the experienced shift boss stated : 'No praise could be too great for the men concerned. I may add that I have been a miner for 28 years and have never seen a braver act.'

Samanu Wangara (40) Head Truck Boy and Benjamin (30) Head Timber Boy were each awarded the Bronze Medal.

Strachan, Peter, (18), Deck Hand　　　　　　　　　　　　　　　　　　　　　　　　　　　　　　　　　　Case 62839

Stanhope Gold Medal 1952

42 miles off Great Yarmouth, Norfolk. At 9.0 p.m. on 27th October, 1952, it then being dark and stormy, the fishing vessel *Three Bells*, sailing from Great Yarmouth, shot its gear in a depth of 22 fathoms. The wind was E.N.E. with gale force, sea exceptionally heavy. This weather, which was bad, now deteriorated to an alarming degree, the wind rising to gale force and increasing. The Skipper gave the order to start hauling in the gear. At this moment a very heavy sea struck the vessel, and the messenger rope jumped out of the cage roller; this threw Mate William George Buchan (59) over the ship's side into the sea.

The chances of rescue are described as:- *a million to one chance that he ever got back to the boat with Buchan, who is a very heavy man and was unconscious* (Caledonian Fishselling and Marine Stores Company, Ltd., of Peterhead), and *the risk was suicidal and generally accepted as such by seafarers in the vicinity* (R Forman, Esq., Magistrate and Baillie of Peterhead). None the less Deck Hand Strachan went in after removing his boots and oilskin. To reach Mate Buchan he had to swim to windward but, with difficulty, he reached and supported the 14 - 15 stone man who was unconscious.

Deck Hand Strachan supported Mate Buchan for 35 minutes, keeping him above the surface of the water in the light of flares and searchlights. On the vessel coming round and closing the two men in the water Mate Buchan was hauled inboard between rolls, followed by Deck Hand Strachan.

Skipper Alex. Strachan of the vessel *Three Bells* states:- *I consider that in all my sea experience I have never seen nor, in fact, heard, of a man being saved in conditions such as prevailed that night.*

Gill, Thomas Frederick, (33), Upholsterer. Fireman Cornwall Fire Brigade　　　　　　　　　Case 62951

Stanhope Gold Medal 1953

Saved Robert James Graham (20), Mining Student. In a disused mine shaft and old workings, Cligga Shaft, Cligga, Perranporth, Cornwall.

On 21st March, 1953, Mr Graham, with a companion, was exploring the old workings at Cligga. After being about 80 feet down for about an hour Mr Graham decided to rejoin his companion who had remained at the top. Mr Graham climbed a rope which was made fast at the top of the shaft but, when five feet from the top, he lost his hold and fell into the shaft, being severely injured in the fall. Mr Graham's companion went for assistance and the Perranporth Unit of the Fire Brigade came to the scene.

On arrival of the Fire Brigade a survey of the position was made. The top of the shaft is guarded with girders 14 inches apart, making the entry impossible to a big man. The Divisional Officer, who was desirous of leading the rescue was unable to squeeze through the obstacle. Mr Graham, who could not be seen from the top, was able to make delirious answers to calls. It being clear that time was too precious to await the removal of the obstacle Fireman Gill volunteered to go down.

About 50 feet down the shaft is a platform of granite from which the working slopes away at an angle of about 50 degrees. Mr Graham was in this. Fireman Gill located him in a chamber of loose and dangerous granite which might slip and cause severe injuries or even death to anyone who entered it and Mr Graham was, as stated, injured.

The ambulance now arrived and Mr Andrew was lowered to the platform and a stretcher was lowered to him. With caution Fireman Gill then went down through the passage of loose granite rocks in the lower working and secured Mr Graham whom he brought to the platform. Mr Graham was bleeding from injuries but was conscious. It was decided that Mr Graham was sufficiently in possession of his faculties to assist in the rescue so morphia was not used. He was put on the stretcher. The position was still of considerable danger as falling rocks and stones endangered all three. Fireman Gill and Mr Andrew accordingly stood over Mr Graham and took the fall of stones on themselves to prevent further injuries to Mr Graham and continued to do this until he was hauled clear. The two salvors were then themselves hauled up. The rescue took from 5.45 - 7.30 p.m. to accomplish.

Richard Henry Andrew received the Bronze Medal.

Shemmedi, Mehmet Mustafa, (19), Porter   Case 63462

Stanhope Gold Medal 1954

In the sea, off Famagusta saved Zenon Christofi (42), Night Guard and attempted to save one woman who died later and two other persons who were found to be dead.

On 25th May, 1953, a Fair was being held in the town. A boat, with a capacity of 16 went out from the Fair with 19 persons on board. About 100 yards out it struck a reef and went down. Those on board were drowned or in danger of drowning. The alarm was given by the Police and Shemmedi entered the water and swam out. It was then 10 p.m. The night was clear with no moon, the sea was choppy and there was a strong wind. After a trying swim out to sea Shemmedi secured an exhausted woman and took her to a fishing boat. He then continued his search for the missing and secured two persons struggling in the sea. One, a man, caught Shemmedi by the leg and compelled the would-be-salvor to release his grasp. Shemmedi then dived again and secured the man who had forced him to let go, getting the man into a boat. The salvor then dived again and searched for the woman but she was dead. Then, being exhausted, he swam ashore.

When on shore, he was told that 2-3 other persons were still unaccounted for. After removing his dripping clothes he swam out to sea to attempt to complete the rescue. On arrival at the wrecked boat he dived again and found a man trapped by his trousers to the engine of the boat. With difficulty Shemmedi released the man who was, however, dead.

Shemmedi was in the water for three hours and, apart from the person actually saved his inspiration resulted to some extent in the saving of 16 out of the 19 persons who went down with the launch.

Beale, Ivor Laurence, (26), Petty Officer (Upper Yardman Air), Royal Navy   Case 63945

Stanhope Gold Medal 1955

Saved Midshipman (Air) Richard William Mile Shepherd (21), Royal Naval Volunteer Reserve. In the sea 20 miles North West of Lands End.

On the night of 24th January, 1955, at 7.0 p.m., a Firefly Mk. 7 aircraft of No. 796 Squadron, attached to the Naval Observer and Air Signal School, R.N.A.S. Culdrose, crashed in the sea 20 miles N.W. of Lands End. The weather was overcast with a force of 4 (11-16 m.p.h.). The wind was S./S.W., moderate sea and swell. The pilot is missing, believed killed and salvor and saved were in the rear cockpit. On crashing the aircraft turned over and sank. Both rear cockpit occupants released themselves from the aircraft under water but Shepherd's dinghy snagged and he had to leave it in the aircraft. Beale escaped with his dinghy and on coming to the surface, spent about 2 minutes releasing his parachute and making sure his dinghy was secure. Then realising that Shepherd was in the water about 50 feet away, without a dinghy, Beale swam to him and then opened his own dinghy. Seeing that Shepherd was injured in the head and only partly conscious, Beale pushed him into the dinghy (designed for one man capacity) and then climbed in himself over Shepherd's legs. Beale's action in rescuing Shepherd and getting him into the dinghy is most praiseworthy in view of the fact that Beale himself had a badly contused arm and a fractured rib, sustained in the crash. (Report of Captain W.W.R. Bentick, R.N. Air Station, Culdrose.) Subsequently in the dinghy Beale attempted to revive Shepherd with his own warmth as Shepherd's immersion suit had been torn in escaping from the aircraft and was full of water; and, when Shepherd had revived, they took it in turns to keep each other warm, Beale having broken the seal of his immersion suit in rescuing Shepherd and so also being wet through. The following statement was made in reply to the Society's questionnaire: Beale in delaying getting into his own dinghy in his injured condition, by going to rescue Shepherd, and in sharing his own one man dinghy with Shepherd, considerably decreased his own chances of survival and rescue.

After three hours of exposure the two men were picked up by the British Tanker *Scottish Eagle*. The Master of the *Scottish Eagle* reported: Referring back to the incident on the night of the 24th inst. I would like the attention of the proper authority drawn to the great bravery shown by U.Y. Beale in saving the life of Midshipman Shepherd. When these two men fought their way out of the aircraft it was submerged to a depth of about 20 feet and both of them were injured and badly shocked. Beale's dinghy, which was the only one to inflate, was, after all, only a one man dinghy and how he managed to get a helpless semi-conscious man into it, in the sea and swell then running, is almost beyond understanding. He could only have managed this by jeopardising his own life. During all the time they were in the water alongside the ship, during the recovery from the water and during removal from the lifeboat to the hospital, Beale's only thought was: For God's sake mind his legs.

A Doctor was transferred from HMS *Triumph* to the *Scottish Eagle*. He treated the survivors for injuries, shock and exposure. The *Scottish Eagle* was diverted to Falmouth where the survivors were landed at 5.30 a.m. on 25th January and transferred to the Sick Bay, RNAS *Culdrose*.

O'Sullivan, Hugh Barry, Lieutenant Colonel, M.C., Royal Tank Regiment   Case 64827
Posthumous Award

Stanhope Gold Medal 1956

Attempted to save Lieutenant David Henry Thomas Blackburn, Royal Tank Regiment, and Michael Morton, both deceased, and saved Mrs Margaret O'Sullivan.

The action took place in the sea, off Culver Cliff, Isle of Wight, on 29th July, 1956 at 1.56 p.m. It was 1 1/3 miles from the shore with a full gale from the South-west blowing. The sea was very rough and those involved were in the water for four hours. The survivors were taken from the water by one of Her Majesty's ships - H.M.S. *Keppel*.

Lieut-Col O'Sullivan was out sailing in a Bermudan sloop with three other people, i.e. Mrs O'Sullivan (his wife), Lt Blackburn and a Mr Morton. A gale sprang up and after a long period of sailing in extremely dangerous weather the sloop broke up and sank, but the dinghy was thrown clear.

Lt-Col O'Sullivan helped and inspired the other three members of the crew while they were hanging on the keel of the dinghy. Mr Morton lost consciousness and Lt-Col O'Sullivan held him on to the dinghy until it was obvious that he was dead.

H.M.S. *Keppel* came to their assistance and saw the three people remaining round the waterlogged dinghy. The wind was a full gale from the S.W. and the sea very rough. Lt-Col O'Sullivan took off his life-jacket to wave to the ship and attract attention. Lt Blackburn drifted away from the dinghy and Lt-Col O'Sullivan hauled him back and continued to support him. The crew of the *Keppel* then took Mrs O'Sullivan aboard but, in the meantime, Blackburn drifted away again and Lt-Col O'Sullivan swam off to try and help him. Because of the state of the wind and the sea the ship drifted away during the rescue of Mrs O'Sullivan and lost sight of Lt-Col O'Sullivan and Lt Blackburn. Despite a search they were unable to find them again. In such a sea Lt-Col O'Sullivan, who left the dinghy to try and help Lt Blackburn, had no chance of surviving for more than a short time, hampered as he was by his oilskins and without his life-jacket. It is considered that his gallant conduct showed complete disregard for his personal safety in attempting to save Lt Blackburn.

Robertson, William, Fisherman   Case 65192

Stanhope Gold Medal 1957

Contributed in a most gallant manner to the saving of the crew of the Seine net fishing boat *Venus Star*. The action took place at sea off Ullapool, Scotland, between midnight and dawn on 22nd July, 1957.

The *Venus Star* landed a catch at Ullapool and sailed for Stornaway, the crew turning in, leaving one of their number at the wheelhouse. At 12.10 a.m. the smell of burning was evident in the wheelhouse which intensified and the crew were turned out. Opening the hatch, a formidable fire was seen in the engine which was a petrol-started Diesel.

Another ship was called by R/T but this went dead. Despite all the efforts of the crew, the fire increased. Course was altered for Ullapool but the ship could not reach this anchorage so an attempt was made to beach her on Gruinard Island but the engine stopped.

It was now decided to abandon ship. A self-inflating raft was launched but the rope securing it to the ship either parted or was burnt and the raft drifted away. Seeing this, Robertson, who is physically handicapped by being deaf and dumb, jumped into the sea and swam to the raft which had drifted some distance away. He attempted to paddle with his hands to the doomed ship but at one time they were 200 yards apart. Eventually the two drifted together and the crew got on the raft.

The Master of the *Venus Star* reported, There is no doubt that the very brave action of Robertson saved all our lives for had the raft drifted away I would have given very little for our chances of survival. The night was cold with a fair breeze blowing from the North and there was quite a lot of motion on the sea. By this time the whole ship was ablaze from stem to stern.

The survivors landed at 7 a.m. near Aultbea, but the ship drifted ashore a total wreck.

Hall, David John Nowell, Lieutenant, Royal Navy   Case 65958

Stanhope Gold Medal 1958

Saved at great risk to his own life, that of an 11-years-old boy. On the night of the 13th September, 1958 the motor yacht *Saint Francis*, on passage from Corfu to Italy, ran into bad weather. The sky was completely overcast with no star visible. It was raining and a fresh wind had caused a short steep sea in which the yacht laboured heavily at a speed of 11 knots. At a few minutes past 10 o'clock. an 11-years -old boy (a passenger) came on deck to be seasick but, as he reached the rail, the ship gave a heavy lurch which flung him over-board.

Luckily a deck-hand saw him go. The engines were immediately stopped and the ship turned down to leeward. Some minutes later the cries of the boy were heard and, for a brief moment, he was sighted at a considerable distance from the ship in the beams of a searchlight; but an attempt to launch the dinghy failed as she broached to, filled with water, stove in her side against the yacht's stern, and sank. Without hesitation Lieutenant David Hall, Royal Navy, dived overboard fully clad and' although not an exceptionally strong swimmer, succeeded in reaching the boy, who was utterly exhausted. Lieut. Hall swam back to the ship with the boy and both were helped aboard since neither had the strength by this time to negotiate a Jacob's ladder. There is no doubt that Lieut Hall's prompt and gallant action saved the boy's life.

In 1962 the Stanhope Gold Medal was made open to the Liverpool Shipwreck and Humane Society (founded 1839), the Royal Humane Society of Australasia (1874), the Royal Shipwreck Relief and Humane Society of New South Wales (1877), the Royal Canadian Humane Association (1894), and the Royal Humane Society of New Zealand (1898).

The official Stanhope Gold Medal citation for the following awards are reproduced in full. Where the Stanhope Gold Medal was voted to recipients who had previously been decorated by Societies other than the RHS, the original citations are reproduced only where they expand upon the details contained in the Stanhope citations.

Jorgensen, Graham Morris, (27), Engineer   No Case Number

Stanhope Gold Medal 1962

Case submitted by Royal Humane Society of Australasia

Just after Christmas 1961 (28th December 1961) a party went swimming at Lamberts Beach, Queensland.

Two young people, an eighteen years old girl and a twenty-four years old man were frolicking in 2-3 feet of water 6-7 yards from the shore. Mr Graham Morris Jorgensen sat on the beach watching. Suddenly, without warning a shark attacked. The shark severed the young man's right hand and forearm and then went for the girl, biting both her arms off and mauling her right leg so badly it had to be amputated.

Mr Jorgensen did not hesitate. He dashed into the sea, beating on the water, and at the shark. He put his head under the water and shouted. The shark withdrew some distance. Jorgensen was then able to get the two young people out of the water. The girl died some time later in hospital.

When submitting this case the Society's Secretary made the following observation - There are several books on skin diving, notably those by Hans Hass, which refer to shouting under water as a possible means of scaring sharks, and we understand from people who have had considerable experience of surfing and life-saving, that it is possible but not a certain method of scaring the shark.

Jorgensen also awarded the Clarke Medal in Gold of the RHSA.

Knight, Frederick John   No Case Number

Stanhope Gold Medal 1963

Case submitted by the Royal Shipwreck Relief and Humane Society of New South Wales

A party of four men and two women went to Sugarloaf Bay and then to North Arm, Middle Harbour, Sydney for the purpose of a picnic. They travelled by motor launch which they moored in deep water and those who wished were ferried ashore in a dinghy. One man remained on the launch.

When they reached the shore the party were enjoying themselves, either wading in the shallow water at the edge or digging for oysters in the also shallow water. Mr Knight and a woman were chipping oysters from rocks in water between knee and thigh deep. Mr Knight was about ten feet from the girl and slightly further out from the shore but with his back to her. He heard her scream and turned round to see her being dragged into deep water with blood colouring the water around her. Without hesitation Mr Knight rushed to the girl and although aware that a shark had hold of her he grabbed her by the arms and tried to pull her from the jaws of the shark. During the struggle he too was pulled into deeper water and he could see that the shark was holding her by the right thigh and pelvic region. In his struggle with the shark Mr Knight found himself astride the shark and he commenced to kick it and punch it with his left hand. Subsequently he was able to release the girl from the jaws of the shark and convey her close to the shore where he was able to touch bottom and call for help. With assistance the girl was carried to the beach where first aid was applied. Later she was taken to hospital but was dead on arrival. The struggle lasted half an hour.

Mr Knight flew back from Lagos where he is now working and the Duke of Gloucester invested him with the Stanhope Gold Medal at 12 noon on 12th March. The simple but moving ceremony took place at St James' Palace in the presence of Mr Knight's mother and brother, the Chairman, Captain A.A. Russell, representing the New South Wales Society, and the Secretary.

Knight also awarded the Silver Medal of the RHS of New South Wales.

Teehu Makimare No Case Number

Stanhope Gold Medal 1964

Case submitted by the Royal Humane Society of New Zealand

On the 12th August, 1963 four pearling cutters set out from Manihiki to sail the twenty five miles of open ocean to the neighbouring and more fertile island of Rakahanga to obtain supplies of green vegetables, fruit and trade goods. One of the boats was the *Tearoha*, a 13 foot cutter partly decked fore and aft carrying a mainsail and jib. Skippering the boat was 43 year old Enoka Dean and with him were Teehu Makimare, 29, Toka Tuhe, 35, Tupou Papai, 33, Kita Marsters, 28, Taia Tauraki, 42, and Tom Tangimetua, 24. The trip to Rakahanga was uneventful and the boats arrived during the afternoon of the same day. On the morning of 15th August the boats were loaded for the return journey. Enoka Dean chose a different course from the other three boats and they were soon out of sight. Head winds and rising seas made it obvious that the boat would not reach Manihiki before dark. The next morning the bowsprit snapped and the jib blew away. The mainsail was then lowered and the boat began to drift before the wind, and it was not until 17th October, 64 days after leaving Rakahanga, that the boat containing four emaciated survivors grounded on Eromanga in the New Hebrides, a distance of over two thousand miles. These survivors were Teehu Makimare, Toka Tuhe, Tupou Papai and Taia Tauraki; but Taia Tauraki died shortly afterwards as a result of his suffering.

Throughout the long journey, Teehu Makimare acted as leader of the group. On 25th September when the boat overturned, Teehu dived below the upturned vessel to free Kita Marsters. He then swam to the floating boom, rolled and tied the sail around it, and managed with the help of his companions, to get Marsters and Tangimetua on the boom. Teehu then gathered and tied together paddles and pieces of timber and placed Tupou Papai upon this makeshift raft. Teehu then called upon Dean, Tauraki and Tuhe to release their holds on the upturned hull and assist him to right the boat. In the heavy seas this was finally accomplished after long hours of endeavour. The men on the boom had drifted away and were not seen again and Dean died some days later.

Throughout the whole voyage Teehu Makimare displayed leadership qualities and courage of the highest order; and his conduct was largely responsible for saving the lives of some of his companions. The sixty-four day drift took the small boat past Tonga and the Fiji Islands two thousand miles.

Teehu Makimare also awarded the Gold Medal of the RHS of New Zealand.

Campbell, Barry John, Lieutenant, 1st Field Regiment, RAFA No Case Number

Stanhope Gold Medal 1965

Case submitted by the Royal Shipwreck Relief and Humane Society of New South Wales.

The Duke of Gloucester awarded the Stanhope Gold Medal 1965 to Lieutenant Barry John Campbell, who at 11.30 a.m. on the 24th March, 1964, on a dangerous height two hundred and fifty feet above the rocky sea shore where there was a strong gusty wind at 'The Gap' Watsons Bay, Sydney, New South Wales, Australia, gallantly saved the life of a young girl who was about to commit suicide and struggled violently when apprehended.

At about 11.30 a.m. on the 24th March, 1964, Lieutenant Campbell (then a Sergeant) was off-duty from his army duties at a Barracks nearby, and was walking in the vicinity of 'The Gap' (some five hundred yards from the Barracks) when he noticed a number of people apparently watching, what he thought, was a souvenir anchor known as the 'Dunbar Anchor'.

He moved to the group and saw a girl, aged 17 years, standing on a projecting ledge of rock outside the safety fence and only two feet from the cliff edge. The group of observers that first attracted his attention were making no efforts to save the girl who apparently was intending suicide.

Campbell approached the girl from behind and sat on a ledge about five feet away from the girl. They were separated by a gap in the rocks. The width of the ledge the girl was on is less than four feet.

At this time a Constable of Police arrived at the scene with a special safety harness and was seen by the girl who at once moved to within one foot of the edge of the cliff. Campbell immediately jumped across the gap to the ledge on which the girl had been sitting, took hold of her bodily, lifted her off the ground and leant back against the cliff edge. The girl struggled violently for several minutes until two Police Officers were able to join Campbell and assist him and the girl to safety.

It has been ascertained that on the morning in question a gusty South West wind was blowing at 10 to 20 knots causing the girl to sway backwards and forwards on the edge of the cliff. This wind made the rescue extremely hazardous.

Campbell also awarded the Bronze Medal of the RHS of New South Wales.

Greengrass, Charles Paul, Chief Petty Officer, Royal Navy, H.M.S. St Angelo   Case 70287

Stanhope Gold Medal 1966

Case submitted by Royal Humane Society

The President of the Royal Humane Society, H.R.H. The Duke of Gloucester, has awarded the 1966 Stanhope Gold Medal to Chief Petty Officer Charles Paul Greengrass, Royal Navy, H.M.S. *St Angelo*, for having on the 22nd October, 1965, at great personal risk gone to the rescue of a man who was in imminent danger of drowning in very rough and turbulent seas off Dragut Point, at Sliema, Malta, G.C., and whose life he gallantly saved, this being the most meritorious case submitted to the Society for the year 1966.

A thirty-two year old man had been swept by heavy seas out of the swimming pool belonging to a Hotel on Dragut Point. H.M.S. *Ashton* and H.M. Tug *Airedale* went to the scene but were unable to effect a rescue because of the heavy sea running and the proximity of a lee shore. M.F.V. (motor fishing vessel) 256 commanded by Lieutenant John Bucksey, Royal Navy, reached the scene and managed to get near enough to the man to throw in a life buoy, which he grabbed. The man was then hauled to the M.F.V.'s side, where it was observed that he was beyond helping himself. Chief Petty Officer Greengrass, Salvor, Jumped over the side to assist the man, who at that moment let go the life buoy and disappeared. Greengrass dived below the surface of the very rough sea and re-appeared with him. At this stage the M.F.V. had been blown perilously close to the rocks and the undertow of the heavy seas caused by the proximity of the rocks swept Greengrass and the saved man down underneath the M.F.V. They re-appeared from under the stern Greengrass still holding the man who was no longer able to help himself at all. Twice more the two men were swept out of sight, and on each occasion, the man was still supported by Greengrass. The violent rolling of the M.F.V., the undertow and general turbulence of the sea made it impossible for anyone on the M.F.V. to assist the two men in the water, who it was feared would both be lost. After three attempts to reach the M.F.V., Greengrass made a last super-human effort and managed with the saved man to get close enough to the M.F.V. to be grabbed and hauled aboard.

An annex to the Society's form states - During the course of this rescue the M.F.V. was being set rapidly onto the rocks of Dragut Point, C.P.O. Greengrass was well aware of this, and that the M.F.V. might have to leave him in consequence, when his chance of recovery by boat would have been slight. He was also well aware that he would have stood little chance of escaping grave injury, or indeed of surviving if the seas had swept him onto the rocks.

Commodore Commanding H.M.S. *St Angelo* states - It is therefore only necessary for me to state that I consider Chief Petty Officer Greengrass's actions to have been well beyond the scope of duty and to warrant immediate recognition. I have also considered the actions of Lieutenant (SD) (B) John Bucksey, Royal Navy, who was in command of the M.F.V. While not qualifying for an award by the Royal Humane Society, I nevertheless consider that this Officer displayed seamanship and resolution of a high order in his handling of the M.F.V. in heavy and confused seas in the close proximity of a dangerous lee shore. I submit that he is worthy of a Commander-in-Chief's commendation.

Admiral Sir John Hamilton, Commander-in-Chief of Mediterranean, states - I consider Chief Petty Officer Greengrass showed exceptional courage and determination in persisting in such difficult and dangerous conditions, in his rescue attempt until it was finally successful. I strongly recommend that his brave action should receive the recognition of a Royal Humane Society award.

C.P.O. Greengrass had a fine last-war record. He joined as a boy in 1939, was sunk in H.M.S. *Edinburgh* in 1942, he then spent two-and-a-half months near Murmansk as a survivor. He next joined H.M.S. *Niger* at Murmansk for return to the United Kingdom. He was sunk again. This time north of Iceland. Greengrass was the last of seven survivors having been in the sea for about half an hour without a lifebelt. Later he served in India and Italy with Combined Operations. He is married with two teenage sons.

Easton, Jack Milne, (22), Junior Engineer, Merchant Navy   Case 70951

Stanhope Gold Medal 1967

Case submitted by Royal Humane Society

At Umm Said, Qatar, Persian Gulf, at 5.25 a.m. on 20th August, 1966, the Tanker *British Crown* was loading crude oil about seven hundred yards from the shore and two hundred yards from the mooring buoy in fifty feet of water. There was an explosion followed by fire which engulfed her amidships, and burning oil spread on the water on the starboard side.

Easton was on watch in the engine room. He encouraged the Indian crew members to jump into the sea, by force where necessary, following them into the water. He swam about the side of the ship looking for survivors and on four occasions swam backwards and forwards between the ship and the mooring buoy (to which survivors made their way) assisting four Indian seamen. At one stage, a blazing launch was drifting down on the buoy, threatening the survivors clinging to it. Easton swam to the launch and pushed it so that it floated past clear of the buoy.

Easton swam anything from twelve hundred yards to a mile or more. Oil was burning on the water, there was the possibility of explosions and sharks.

Easton also awarded the Mountbatten Medal of the Royal Life Saving Society.

Ryan, Robert John, (23)   No Case Number

Stanhope Gold Medal 1968

Case submitted by the Royal Humane Society of New Zealand.

On the 14th February, 1968 at great personal risk saved the life of one man and attempted to save the life of another in a deep crevasse of melting snow and ice on a glacier at Silberhorn Ridge, Mount Cook National Park, New Zealand.

While climbing a man slipped and dragging a second man with him, slid towards the Linda Glacier for about 500 feet. The two men, who were roped together, then fell into a crevasse (shrund) some 60 feet deep. One died of his injuries before help could arrive, but the other crawled to the edge of the crevasse from where he hoped to be visible to a rescue party. As he waited, ice and snow were breaking off and falling round him.

The other members of the party went to fetch help and in due course Ryan and an assistant arrived on the scene. Belayed on a 120 foot rope by the assistant, Ryan descended into the crevasse which was situated on the upward slope not far from the edge of an ice-cliff some 500 feet high. The crevasse was showing signs of being about to collapse. Ryan reached the first man and confirmed he was dead.

Ryan then called to the second. The latter replied that he could not return; but that he could be lowered from where he was at the edge of the crevasse. Ryan having run out of rope (120 feet) detached himself from the safety of the rope, and made his way along the crevasse to him. He made things more secure for them both by the use of ice screws and pitons, and arranged a type of chair with the man's own rope. Ryan was then able to lower him down the ice face to a point which had been reached by a second rescue party 100 feet below. Ryan was in this dangerous situation for about one and a half hours, at the end of which time the ice was cracking more frequently. Almost immediately after he left the place from which he lowered the man, the whole of that section collapsed, narrowly missing the stretcher party below; But Ryan was able to hold onto the ice screws. With help from his assistant, Ryan cut steps in the wall of the crevasse and regained the ridge.

Both Ryan and his assistant knew the area was a dangerous one for avalanches and both realised the risk caused by falling ice and snow. The bravery of both and the skill and experience of Ryan in particular saved one life. Two days later the whole area of ice wall collapsed.

Ryan also awarded the Silver Medal of the RHS of New Zealand.

Broekmeulen, John Christopher, (14), Sea Scout   No Case Number

Stanhope Gold Medal 1970

Case submitted by the Royal Humane Society of Australasia

Three Sea Scouts were swimming across the Swan River, East Perth, Western Australia. Christopher Broekmeulen, aged fourteen, had just reached the bank when a shark attacked his fifteen year old friend, who was some twenty yards behind him. The attacked boy was badly bitten in the leg and pulled under. (He later required more than a hundred stitches in the wound). Hearing the cry for help Christopher encouraged the third lad, who seemed to be initially so shocked as to have been unable to move, to swim to the side. While he himself ran back into the water and swam out to where the blood on the water could clearly be seen.

Christopher reached the badly injured boy, turned him on his back and swam with him to the bank and safety.

Broekmeulen also awarded the Clarke Medal in Silver of the RHS of Australasia. The citation is as follow:

CLARK SILVER MEDAL - 7861
JOHN CHRISTOPHER BROEKMEULEN, Mt. Lawley, (W.A.), aged 14 years, in going to the rescue of Graham Cartwright, aged 15 years, who was attacked by a shark in the Swan River, East Perth, on 29th November, 1969.

About 3 p.m. four sea scouts were swimming in the river which was fairly dirty and warm. They swam across the river, 140 yards, and later, three swam back again. Broekmeulen swam ahead and reached the beach when the others were about 20 yards out. Cartwright suddenly called out for help because he had been bitten. Broekmeulen immediately ran back into the water. Visibility in the water was nil but as he got nearer he could see the water was red with blood. He reached Cartwright, put his arm under his chin, and swam with him to the shore. He then tried to stop the bleeding until the assistant scout master took over. The third swimmer saw the shark as it attacked, but it was not seen again.

Nicol, Thomas, (13), Schoolboy   Case 73455

Stanhope Gold Medal 1971

Case submitted by Royal Humane Society

PLACE/ TIME:	Dancing Cairns Quarry, Aberdeenshire. 29th March 1971. 6 pm.
CONDITIONS:	The quarry has drops of up to 80 feet. Salvor jumped down 10 feet, then dived 32 feet into bitterly cold water, only 5 or 6 feet deep. The water had sunken debris and a number of underwater rocks.
SALVOR:	Thomas NICOL (13) Schoolboy.
ASSISTANT:	Kenneth NICOL (11) Schoolboy
SAVED:	Alison FRASER (5)
SUMMARY:	While playing at the edge of the quarry with another girl the SAVED little five year-old fell over the edge, down 40 feet into the water, bouncing on a protruding rock on the cliff face en route.

Thomas and Kenneth NICOL, who were nearby, saw this happen. In fact Thomas had previously warned the little girls they should not be playing there. Thomas NICOL, (aged 13) quickly jumped down about 10 feet from the spot where the girl had fallen, on to a lower ledge of the cliff. He then dived down 32 feet into the water (5 or 6 feet deep) which abounded in sunken rocks and debris.

He swam till he found the little girl under water, then brought her to the surface, and the side. Kenneth NICOL helped get the child out and they both dragged the bleeding child up the cliff face. She has since recovered and is out of hospital.

Testimonial on vellum to Kenneth Nicol.

Aspeslet, Malcom Rodney   No Case Number

Stanhope Gold Medal 1972

Case submitted by the Royal Canadian Humane Association

It was decided to recommend the Canadian entry for the 1972 Stanhope Gold Medal. The President therefore awarded the Stanhope Gold Medal to Malcolm Aspeslet for saving the life of a girl from the attack of a female grizzly bear with cubs on 1st October 1971. The detailed story is as follows :-

Mr Aspeslet and his companion Miss Barbara Beck both aged eighteen, were hiking along a trail in Glacier National Park, when on rounding a bend they came across a female grizzly bear and her two cubs. The bear was on all fours but then it stood up to a height of six feet, snorted, grunted and charged.

The girl either fell or was thrown to the ground and Aspeslet tried to protect her with his body; but the bear threw him aside and attacked the girl. Aspeslet then jumped on the bear's back and proceeded to stab her with his hunting knife. The bear left the girl and fought with Aspeslet. Aspeslet yelled to the girl to feign dead and he and the bear wrestled on the ground rolling down a twenty foot embankment.

Aspeslet was very badly mauled, but at this point the grizzly seemed to remember her cubs and left him. Miss Beck, though she suffered cuts to her head and shoulders, managed to walk two and a half mile to report what had happened. A party then went out in a helicopter to bring Aspeslet in. he required considerable hospital treatment.

Aspeslet also awarded the Star of Courage (Canada), the Gold Medal of the Royal Canadian Humane Association, the Bronze Medal of the Carnegie Hero Fund (N. America) and the Gold Medal for Saving Life (Alberta).

Starr, Abraham, (33), Department of Indian Affairs   No Case Number

Stanhope Gold Medal 1974

Case submitted by the Royal Canadian Humane Association

PLACE/ TIME:	From a fire in a house at Heron Bay Indian Reserve, Ontario, Canada. 3rd May, 1973.
CONDITIONS:	An inferno of intense heat and smoke.
SALVOR:	Abraham STARR (33) Department of Indian Affairs. A Canadian Indian.
SAVED:	Rachel FISHER (3)
	Larry Francis FISHER (1)
	Daphne FISHER (2 months) - DECEASED
SUMMARY:	A house fire completely destroyed the home of Larry FISHER at the Heron Bay Indian Reserve. At the time of the fire, FISHER was at work and his wife was at a neighbour's home.

Abraham STARR noticed smoke coming from the house and was told there were children in it. STARR entered the burning house and, hampered by heat and dense smoke, crawled to a bedroom. He located two of FISHER's children aged three and one. He rescued them from the house.

Once outside with these children, their mother told STARR that her two month old daughter was sleeping in another bedroom in the house. STARR again entered the house; but was unable to locate the third child due to intense heat and smoke. STARR was deeply distressed over the infant who died in the inferno.

Starr also awarded the Star of Courage (Canada) and the Silver Medal of the Royal Canadian Humane Association.

Gleeson, Terry Haydon, (22), Boiler-welder   No Case Number

Stanhope Gold Medal 1975

Case submitted by the Royal Humane Society of Australasia

... to Terry Haydon Gleeson of Queensland, Australia, for his gallant attempts to save the life of a man after an explosion inside the buoyancy chamber of a tidal marker buoy on the 5th October, 1974.

Gleeson also awarded the Clarke Medal in Silver of the RHS of Australasia. The citation is as follow:

CLARKE SILVER MEDAL - 8297
TERRY HAYDON GLEESON, Cairns (Q.), boiler-welder, aged 22 years, in going to the rescue of a man following an explosion in a buoyancy chamber on 5th October, 1974.

About 10.15 a.m. two men were painting the interior of a tidal marker buoy with highly inflammable paint, when there was an explosion. One man was in the tunnel leading to the buoyancy chamber at the time and was able to crawl to the entrance where he was helped by workmates. He was hysterical and very badly burned. Smoke and fumes were coming from the tunnel. Gleeson tried to get through the manhole of the first section of the chamber but the fumes were too strong, so he turned back, exchanged the lead light for a torch and changed the air hose. He then crawled back into the first section with the torch and air hose but the man was not there. He put the air hose through the manhole in an effort to clear the fumes and could see the man lying unconscious on his side. His overalls were burnt off him and he was burnt all over. Gleeson tried to pull him to the manhole but his skin kept peeling off in his hands and his foot seemed to be jammed somewhere. His own breathing became very difficult and he realised that he could not rescue the man on his own. He could not feel a pulse and believed the man was dead. When he tried to crawl out his legs appeared to be paralysed and he had to pull himself along pipes inside the tunnel. Gleeson was taken to hospital and required treatment for three months for his paralysis trouble and nerves. The man was eventually rescued by workmen cutting open the chamber, but he died the next day without regaining consciousness. Gleeson's effort lasted about half an hour.

Robson, Graham Thomas, (23), Police Constable   No Case Number

Stanhope Gold Medal 1976

Case submitted by the Royal Humane Society of Australasia

... to Police Constable Thomas Robson of Camooweal, Queensland, Australia. On the 29th February, 1976, Robson, at great personal risk, saved the life of a man stranded by flood waters in remote and inaccessible area north-east of Camooweal. To effect the rescue, the salvor had to make an extremely hazardous journey on foot and swimming over 40 miles through jungle territory and swollen creeks.

Robson also awarded the Silver Medal of the RHS of Australasia. The citation is as follows:

SILVER MEDAL - 8384
GRAHAM THOMAS ROBSON, Camooweal, (Q), police officer aged 23 years, in undertaking a hazardous journey on foot across flooded country to obtain help for two men stranded in bogged vehicles, on 20 February, 1976.

A man who had been missing for several days was located by a light plane. His vehicle was bogged and he was surrounded by water 100 miles from Camooweal. Robson and a police sergeant set out in the police vehicle and reached the stranded man at 9 p.m. Endeavouring to free the bogged vehicle, the police vehicle also became hopelessly bogged and their efforts until 1 a.m. were fruitless. Realising their dangerous position in flooded country and the possibility of further rain, Robson volunteered to go to Gregory Downs (40 miles) on foot to obtain rescue. It was generally very dark but there was patchy moonlight. After six miles he had to swim Police Creek, which was in full flood, over six feet deep, 80 yards wide with logs and other debris.

The next ten miles was flooded country with water at times knee deep, and boggy ground. Shallow water often disguised irregularities in the surface leading to deeper holes. He suffered considerable discomfort from leeches and chafing from wet and muddy clothes was conscious of possible danger from wild pigs and snakes. At 10 a.m. he topped a rise and saw a grader working in the distance. He waited for it to reach him and was taken the last five miles to Gregory Downs. By now he was very hot and he was exhausted. A rescue party was organised and it reached the bogged vehicles at 4 p.m. The vehicles were freed and the police officers reached Camooweal with the rescued man at midnight.

Davey, Randy Sherman, (19)   No Case Number

Stanhope Gold Medal 1977

Case submitted by the Royal Canadian Humane Association

PLACE/ TIME:	A fire at 70 Main Street, Picton, Ontario, Canada. 24th March, 1977. 12.59 am.
SALVOR:	Randy Sherman DAVEY (19) Unemployed
ASSISTANT:	Kenneth NICOL (11) Schoolboy
SAVED:	Peter Anthony BEIMERS (19)
	Debra Merie GREER
	Mrs Patti Lee SAMUEL
SUMMARY:	DAVEY was driving a car in which there were others, when he saw flames coming from the building of 70 Main Street. (Trent Valley Vending Ltd.)

He drove up to the building, jumped from his car, and ran up the rear stairway to the hallway, (landing) on the second floor. This stairway was completely engulfed in flames. On reaching the second floor hallway (landing) DAVEY banged on the walls and yelled for people to get out. Flames were now following him down the hallway, and DAVEY was burnt on the back of the head, face, hands, and back.

DAVEY forced open the door of Apartment No. 1 and raised the alarm. He smashed the window, and the two occupants and DAVEY jumped onto the lower roof of an adjacent building and to safety. On reaching the ground DAVEY went below the window of another Apartment and talked a pregnant woman into dropping into his arms. DAVEY received first, second and third degree burns to the back of his head, face, and hands, and on his back. The Royal Canadian Humane Association points out that this young man ran grave risks to save complete strangers, (he did not even come from Picton) from certain death. All the witnesses confirm DAVEY definitely saved their lives.

Davey also awarded the Star of Courage (Canada) and the Silver Medal of the Royal Canadian Humane Association.

Howard, Ian Richard   No Case Number

Stanhope Gold Medal 1978

Case submitted by Liverpool Shipwreck & Humane Society

On the 15 October, 1977 Howard ,at great personal risk, saved the life of a man, and attempted to save the life of another, trapped in a burning car on the A565 road at Ince Blundell, Merseyside at 0210 hours. The summary of this brave deed was as follows :-

A young woman was driving along the Formby by-pass towards Liverpool. She was overtaken by a car which appeared to go out of control. It mounted the nearside verge and crashed into a ditch 7ft. below road level. She immediately stopped, but could not get down to the car because of the steepness of the ditch and darkness. She saw that the doors were still shut and that flames were coming from the engine. She attempted to flag down three cars without success and realising that help was imperative, she drove to a house about a quarter of a mile to call out the emergency services.

Howard, who was staying at the house, returned to the accident with the young woman. By then the engine was well ablaze and flames were spreading under the dashboard to the car's interior. One of the occupants, who had apparently been uninjured, had pulled clear the driver and was assisted by others in the process of pulling clear another passenger.

Howard, seeing that there were still two passengers, one in the front seat another in the back, climbed into the car through the nearside rear window. He saw, in the light of the flames, that the rear seat passenger's legs were trapped under the front seat. He pushed the front seat and its occupant towards the windscreen with his feet and freed him with his hands. Assisted by others outside the car, they managed to get him out through a window and removed to safety. It was subsequently discovered he had a broken neck and was paralysed from the waist downwards.

The fire in the car was by now well established, particularly in the front area. Burning plastic from the roof was dripping on the unconscious front passenger's legs. Howard tried to free him by pulling him over the front seat into the back but he was caught. With the help of others, outside the car, Howard pulled and pushed until the man's arm and head were out of one of the car's rear windows. A sudden flare up of the flames and smoke forced the helpers outside to jump back, and Howard had to scramble through the other rear window. The passenger was on fire from the waist down, his hair alight. The back of the car was by now engulfed in flames and the petrol tank was in imminent danger of exploding.

The police arrived moments later when the car was burning fiercely from front to rear. Any attempt at rescue was by then out of the question. The police subsequently reported that any rescue from a fire of such ferocity reflected great credit on the courage and bravery of those involved.

Howard also awarded the Bronze Fire Medal of the LSHS.

McPherson, Bruce Walter, (20)   No Case Number

Stanhope Gold Medal 1979

Case submitted by Royal Humane Society of New South Wales

On the 10th January, 1979 McPherson, at great personal risk, attempted to save the life of a man trapped in a fishing trawler, in dangerous seas, at Yamba Bay, New South Wales. The summary of this brave deed is as follows :-

At about 10 a.m. on 10th January, 1979 the owner/skipper of a 22 metre trawler, *Sea Dreamer*, together with McPherson, put to sea from Yamba for the purpose of trying to salvage an overturned power boat which had capsized on the Yamba Bar area at 7.45 a.m. This salvage attempt continued for about 5-6 hours before the capsized boat was brought to Convent Beach area, then the "Sea Dreamer" commenced to come back to Yamba Port.

It was about 3 p.m. when the trawler was coming into the entrance after the two men had discussed the best way in, owing to the dangerous conditions prevailing at that time. The northern approach was decided on, and the trawler started to steam in. It was then that a large wave appeared from 'nowhere' and started to carry the trawler for about 50 yards, before she broached to the port side, when the water smashed the windows, throwing the skipper away from the wheel and throwing him on to the top of the focsle head steps. He suffered a severe injury, a big cut across the back, which would have immobilised him.

The trawler was hit by several more large waves, gradually filled with water, which was mixed with diesel fuel and leaking refrigeration gas. McPherson made one attempt to get out but the ice box had been pushed against the door, together with copper wires and refrigeration pipes. He managed to get to an air pocket, made another dive and eventually cleared the entrance and swam to the surface.

McPherson then made two separate dives, one down the port side and one down the starboard side of the boat in an attempt to locate the skipper and bring him to the surface. Both these attempt could only be described as extremely dangerous, hazardous and attempted in the most courageous manner. Many dangers presented themselves whilst he was diving, such as leaking refrigeration gas, ropes, wire, debris coming to the surface, turmoil underwater and the possibility of the boat moving in any direction and falling on top of him. There is always the ever present danger of sharks, which constantly frequent the bar area searching for fish coming out of the entrance, as well as following trawlers whenever they work outside.

McPherson eventually located the skipper on the port side and dragged him out, unconscious, to the surface and under much difficulty, pulled him on to the floating ice box. The skipper was covered in diesel fuel and it made him extremely difficult to handle. McPherson then attempted to give him mouth to mouth resuscitation but was unsuccessful as his lungs were full of water and diesel fuel. McPherson was of the opinion that he was dead as he was blue, and a period of about nine minutes had elapsed.

A surf rescue boat had been alerted and after much difficulty negotiating the enormous sea, it managed to reach the two men on the ice box and convey them to another trawler in the vicinity.

McPherson also awarded the Silver Medal of the RHS of New South Wales. The citation includes the following additional details relating to the later stages of the rescue:

… At this time two members of the Yamba Life Saving Club - Messrs. O'Loughlin and Howard - had been alerted and proceeded to the scene in the Club's rubber surf rescue boat. Under very dangerous conditions, they eventually reached the ice-box and transferred Mr. McPherson and his skipper into their rubber craft. A trawler, skippered by Mr. Busch, headed for the north side of the Bar and awaited the arrival of the surf rescue boat which was manoeuvring through debris and huge seas. Mr McPherson and the body of his skipper were placed aboard the trawler. Mr. McPherson spent six days in hospital recovering from the effects of inhaling refrigeration gas and diesel fumes.

Certificates of Merit were awarded by the RHS of New South Wales to Mr. Frank O'LOUGHLIN (50), Mr. Martin Ross HOWARD (27) and Mr. Ronald Peter BUSCH (43).

McNab, John, Station Officer, Mersyside Fire Service   No Case Number

Stanhope Gold Medal 1980

Case submitted by Liverpool Shipwreck & Humane Society

On the 17 July, 1979, McNab, at great personal risk, saved the life of a man threatening suicide from a 150 foot crane on a city centre building site in Liverpool. The summary of this brave deed is as follows :-

A man had just been committed to the Liverpool Crown Court for an offence. He developed an intense hatred of policemen, became mentally distressed, and climbed up numerous ladders on a "Tyson" tower crane situated on a building site at Derby Square, Liverpool. From a position some 150 feet above the ground he shouted to onlookers that he was going to jump. Two police officers started to climb the access ladders, but were obliged to stop and even go back down as the man threatened to throw a metal tool box at them. His experience as a scaffolder was reflected in his confident and agile climbing ability - at one point he had gone out along the jib at the top of the crane structure - and this, together with his violent disposition and loud declarations of hate for all policemen, made him a daunting proposition.

McNab then started to climb the numerous vertical ladders, and as he got nearer to the man's level he too was subjected to the threat of attack from above, but he held his ground and called out that he was a fireman and not a policeman. This had the required effect eventually of quietening him down a bit, and the fire officer continued to talk quietly to him as he edged upwards. He offered him a cigarette, and for several minutes the two men stood one above the other on the crane structure about 150 feet up.

Something then caused the man to lose his temper again, and menacing the fireman with the metal box he still carried, the man climbed further up the crane and went into the crane driver's cabin. McNab followed him, trying to calm him by talking quietly to him all the time, and eventually the man agreed to let him join him in the cabin.

McNab sat quietly on the floor and talked to the man for 20 minutes, during which time he was threatened with a pointed scaling hammer which he brandished over his head from time to time. Despite the frequent references of his ability to bury the hammer in McNab's head, he sat quietly and continued to talk to the man, and finally calmed him down completely and led him down the ladders to the ground where he was arrested.

McNab also awarded the Silver General Medal of the LSHS.

Kalms, Dulcie No Case Number

Stanhope Gold Medal 1981

Case submitted by Royal Humane Society of New South Wales

On the 16th November 1980, Mrs. Kalms courageously saved the lives of four young people trapped in a blazing car east of Temora. The summary of this deed of bravery is as follows:-

A car driven by a young woman ran off the road and collided with a heavy steel telegraph pole and on impact burst into flames. At the time the car contained four young people.

Mrs. Kalms, who resides in a house on a nearby property was awakened by a noise like a large explosion. She went to her bedroom window and saw a motor vehicle against a steel pole on the other side of the main road. She also noticed that the headlights were still turned on and the flames were coming from the front of the vehicle. She then went to another room and woke her daughter and instructed her to ring for the Ambulance and Police and then ran to the scene of the accident, some 150 metres.

On arriving at the scene Mrs. Kalms saw a girl lying in the grass beside the offside rear door and a young man standing beside the vehicle near the girl. She grabbed the girl and dragged her away from the burning vehicle to a grassed area to the rear of the car. She then went to the near side front door where she saw through the window a young man who appeared to be seated in the passenger seat but slumped across another girl who appeared to be wedged under the steering wheel. Both these people seemed lifeless with no movement or sound. As she could not open this door she hurried round the back of the vehicle to the off side door. This door could not be opened but the window was down and she leant through the open window and grabbed the man and commenced to pull him towards the opening. He then seemed to rouse and with his assistance he was removed from the vehicle through the window. After he fell to the ground she found that he could not stand due to his injuries so she pulled him through the fence and induced him to crawl to safety.

Mrs. Kalms then saw that the front of the car was well alight and she again leant through the window and attempted to pull the injured girl out. The girl was wedged under the steering wheel and had her seat belt on. Mrs. Kalms struggled to release the seat belt and by this time the flames were beginning to burn around the legs of the girl. At this time the girl began screaming and moving and she was released from the belt and dragged to safety through the open window. The grass around the car was well alight so Mrs. Kalms returned and dragged the first girl also to safety from the car. Not long after the rescue of the young people the petrol tank exploded and the whole vehicle was engulfed in flames. Mrs. Kalms suffered a slight burn to her left arm, and the young people recovered after two months in hospital.

Kalms also awarded the Silver Medal of the RHS of New South Wales.

Kaleak, Joseph No Case Number

Stanhope Gold Medal 1982

Case submitted by the Royal Canadian Humane Association

On the 25th March 1982 Mr. Kaleak courageously attempted to save the life of a man in a blizzard on Herschel Island, Yukon. The summary of this deed of bravery is as follows:-

A party of five American citizens were on a snow machine from Barter Island, Alaska, to Aklavik, N.W.T., a distance of 400 kms. At a point near Herschel Island, Yukon, in the afternoon of March 25th, 1982, Kaleak and a man separated from the group to view the Island with the intention of rejoining the others at Shingle Point, Yukon. They were travelling on the ice between the mainland and the Island when they were caught in a ground blizzard. Kaleak was towing a sled with all their supplies, knew the way and was leading the man.

They became separated in the whiteout blizzard, and the blowing snow quickly covered all signs of the trail. Kaleak began to search for his companion. For more than two days he kept circling, picking up the man's trail, following it and losing it again. Kaleak did not stop to camp or eat, as he knew his friend had no food, fluid or shelter with him. He continued his search and on the afternoon of the 27th, he was able to locate the man some 100 kms. from where they had separated. Kaleak was weak from his ordeal when he found the man huddled by his snow machine, alive, but unable to move as he was slowly freezing to death. Kaleak set up his tent and burned parts of his sleigh in a vain attempt to assist the man. The man said nothing during the next hours and could not, or would not eat or drink. Kaleak sat up with him through the night, until he died about noon the next day.

He then transported his deceased companion back to Komakuk Beach, the D.E.W. Line Site, a trip of some five hours. This was the nearest location where any other human beings could be found. Kaleak was quite ill from his ordeal and suffered frequent bouts of vomiting through lack of food and sleep. He was sent by a privately chartered aircraft to Aklavik Nursing Station for treatment.

Kaleak also awarded the Silver Medal of the Royal Canadian Humane Association.

Jury, Stephen, (16), student   No Case Number

Stanhope Gold Medal 1983

Case submitted by the Royal Humane Society of Australasia

On the 7th February, 1983 Stephen Jury gallantly rescued a man on the railway track at Boronia Station, Victoria. The summary of this brave deed is as follows:-

Jury was standing on the platform waiting to catch a train on his first day, at a new school. On the platform were some 150 to 200 intending passengers. As the whistle of the approaching train was heard, when it was about 200 metres from the station, the crowd started to move towards the platform edge. Saved was seen to be unsteady and then appeared to faint, falling forward from the platform on to the railway tracks below, and lie unconscious between the tracks, in the path of the oncoming train, now 100 to 120 metres from him.

Jury immediately jumped down on to the tracks and began struggling to lift the man clear. In the space of only five seconds available to him, Jury was able to drag, and lie him against the retaining wall of the platform. The train driver, travelling at about 60 kilometres per hour, saw the figure fall on to the track, then Jury jump down and try to lift and roll Saved clear. He applied the train's brakes in emergency and began blowing the train whistle in a continuous blast. As the front of the train was almost on the site of the fall, he saw Saved lying face-down against the platform wall and Jury throw himself on top of Saved, as both went from his view under the train. The train stopped approximately three carriage lengths beyond the site. The stationmaster then jumped down to render any assistance, and found Jury and Saved safe. The space available between the platform wall and the bogies, and electrical components of the train at track level, is 30 to 40 centimetres.

Saved was taken to hospital for treatment to cuts and abrasions to his feet and face as a result of the fall. One of Jury's shoes was dragged off by the train as it clipped his foot.

Jury's main concern was that he would be late on his first day at a new school.

Jury also awarded the Clarke Medal in Silver of the RHS of Australasia.

Golding, Victor Leonard   79166

Stanhope Gold Medal 1984

Case submitted by Royal Humane Society

On 22nd August 1983, Victor Golding gallantly rescued a man after an explosion at a chemical works in Canning Road, London.. The summary of this brave deed is as follows:-

Salvor and Saved were both on the retort floor of the Nitre Cake Plant (one floor up) to investigate why No. 2 retort was not reaching the usual temperature for a successful operation. The retort suddenly exploded, subjecting Salvor and Saved to acid burns, danger of falling debris and fire, which had started in the wooden roof. Salvor, painfully injured, and in danger of a further explosion and structural collapse of the building, made his way to Saved, injured physically and probably mentally (Hysterical), and by persuasion led and guided him to the ground floor and away from the building. Salvor removed all of Saved's acid contaminated clothing, and washed away and diluted the corrosive acid by dowsing him with water from a hose pipe. He also applied bicarbonite (sic) of soda paste to Saved until the arrival of an ambulance.

Salvor's next main concern was to ensure the safety of the plant for the fire fighters. He courageously returned to the plant, isolated the gas supply and realising the danger from a 500 gallon sulphuric acid header above the roof, whose fractured lines were spraying acid in the area of a retort, isolated the very volatile liquid. In these tasks he exposed himself to injury from flying glass, spraying acid and falling debris. Furthermore, he also drained the header tank, after firstly freeing the valve to the feed lines.

Salvor was suffering from severe shock and was eventually persuaded to go to hospital, although according to witnesses he was more concerned about Saved's condition and the safety of the plant than he was about himself. Salvor received "spotting" acid burns to face, neck, body and legs, all of which he treated himself. He also suffered a cut leg, bruising and severe shock. The fire brigade withdrew at 04.15 hrs.

Garner, David Michael   No Case Number

Stanhope Gold Medal 1985

Case submitted by Liverpool Shipwreck & Humane Society

A girl screaming for help awakened the Salvor and he looked out of the window of his second floor flat. He saw the girl from the flat below leaning out of her window, from which smoke was coming, and he thought she was going to jump. He telephoned the Fire Brigade, dressed quickly and ran downstairs to the flat below.

Kicking open the door, Salvor went into the flat which was full of thick smoke. He could see that the living room was well ablaze, and had to run through this room to get into the back bedroom where the girl was trapped. She was reluctant to leave her bedroom, being afraid of the smoke and flames in the living room, and Salvor was obliged to drag her out and take her downstairs and on to the street. Salvor then re-entered the house and kicked open the door of the ground floor flat, which he knew to be occupied by an 85-year-old man. Smoke from the fire above was already filling the hallway of this flat, and Salvor found the elderly gentleman asleep in his bed. Salvor awakened him and led him outside, and then went back inside again to close the doors of the young woman's flat so that the fire would not spread to his own accommodation above.

Merseyside Fire Brigade extinguished the fire, and made a thorough search wearing breathing apparatus. Considerable damage had been done to the living room by the fire, and the rest of the flat was smoke damaged.

Garner also awarded the Bronze Fire Medal of the LSHS.

Sonnichsen, Gordon William, Pastor   No Case Number

Stanhope Gold Medal 1986

Case submitted by the Royal Canadian Humane Association

On 23 January 1986 Sonnichsen rescued two children from a burning house in St Pierre, Manitoba.

Both saved were having their morning nap when fire broke out in their bedroom. Upon checking the bedroom, their mother found flames three feet high in the middle of the floor. After attempting to enter the room on two separate occasions and being forced back by the smoke and flames, she ran into the hall to set off the fire alarm and alert other occupants of the building.

A neighbour attempted to enter the bedroom but was driven back by thick oily smoke. Other neighbours in the building alerted Salvor, the Pastor at the Bible Fellowship Church which was located next door.

Upon learning that the children were still in the building, Salvor smashed the window leading to their room. Crawling through the smoke and flames and unable to breathe, he immediately came back outside. He again crawled into the bedroom and felt along the walls but could not find the children. He stumbled back and was advised that the children were in a crib located against the wall. The third time he went in, he located one child and handed her to one of the neighbours. He went back the fourth time and located the youngest child and brought her to safety. Two of the neighbours, carrying the badly burned children, ran with them to the local hospital. Unfortunately, the babies died at the hospital, but Salvor had risked his life to get the children out of the inferno.

During the rescue attempts, Salvor was forced to hold his breath. The Fire Chief indicated that he had never witnessed or heard of anyone attempting a feat as was displayed by Salvor without injury or possibly fatal results. He further stated that if Salvor had taken a breath, he would have died from the toxic fumes. Minor scrapes and cuts to both hands and shins were sustained by Salvor while he was breaking the window and crawling over the window frame which was covered with broken glass.

Sonnichsen also awarded the Star of Courage (Canada) and the Silver Medal of the Royal Canadian Humane Association.

Smith, James George   No Case Number

Stanhope Gold Medal 1987

Case submitted by Liverpool Shipwreck & Humane Society

An Edinburgh-London motor coach carrying about 40 passengers and travelling about 50 to 70 mph ploughed into a line of cars and vans held up by lane closures on the M6 southbound carriageway at Barton, Preston. In all thirteen vehicles were crushed, turned round and round or tossed several feet into the air and many of them burst into flames. Fire broke out also in the front of the coach where three passengers died instantly. Slowly the smoke started to spread down the coach and the remaining passengers made for the emergency rear exit door, from where there was a 4ft drop to road level. The emergency door was opened and the solid mass of people in the aisle began pushing those in front. Many fell awkwardly and hurt themselves as others fell onto them, and there was an immediate desire to get as far away as possible from the coach. By the time the last few passengers reached the rear of the coach, much of it was ablaze and it was full of smoke from end to end.

This was the situation which greeted SALVOR when he stopped his northbound journey and ran across the motorway lanes to the scene. It looked like a battlefield and it was difficult to know where to start, but he heard that there might still be some passengers in the coach and he went to it to see if he could help. He observed that its engine was still running and that it was on fire from the front. He found an emergency cut-out button at the back of the coach and pressed it to stop the engine. The rear side exit door was closed and SALVOR reached up and turned the handle. He opened the door and saw a clear air space of about 2 feet at floor level and just inside the door was an unconscious man. SALVOR reached inside and dragged the man out. He than carried him to the central reservation where there was a group of people and leaving the man there SALVOR returned to the coach.

Somehow the door had closed and he re-opened it and looked inside. Collapsed on the floor of the aisle he saw another male figure and, crawling into the coach, he dragged this man to safety. SALVOR then crawled inside the coach again and made his way forward past the second or third seat from the door. The smoke was so thick that he could not see a thing in front of him, but his hands felt another body on the floor of the aisle and he dragged this person out of the coach. It was a male, and SALVOR ensured that others were on hand to apply resuscitation and/ or first aid.

The entire length of the coach was engulfed in flames now and it was impossible for anybody to go near it, so SALVOR went to other vehicles which had been involved in the accident to see if there was anything more he could do.

SALVOR was later taken to hospital where he was treated for shock and smoke inhalation and detained overnight.

Thirteen people died in the accident, three from the coach and ten from cars struck by the coach, but those rescued by SALVOR all recovered after resuscitation and hospital treatment. One of the persons rescued by SALVOR was not a coach passenger but another rescuer who collapsed in the aisle from smoke inhalation when the emergency door closed behind him somehow and he was unable to open it.

Smith also awarded the Silver Fire Medal of the LSHS.

Novis, Rupert, (20), Officer Cadet   Case 80567

Stanhope Gold Medal 1988

Case submitted by the Royal Humane Society

PLACE/ TIME:	River Zambesi above Mana Pools Camp, Zimbabwe. 1st May 1986 (sic). 15.00 hrs. approx.
CONDITIONS:	See Summary.
SALVOR:	Rupert NOVIS (20) Officer Cadet
SAVED:	Jeremy LLOYD (13) Schoolboy
SUMMARY:	A canoe safari party, with a qualified guide, were spending the penultimate day of their safari on the river 8 kms. above their camp. The party consisted of 4 canoes, 2 persons per canoe, including the guide.

The party was drifting downstream in shallow water with 6 members swimming nearby. The guide was in the river holding the canoes. SAVED was swimming furthest upstream when he was suddenly pulled underwater. He was then thrust out of the water in the jaws of a crocodile. SALVOR, who was nearest to saved, threw himself towards the crocodile but SAVED was taken under again before he could reach him.

SALVOR was joined by a member of the party and they both groped about under the water searching for SAVED. This man was also pulled under by the crocodile twisting and turning and was eventually released with a broken and bitten arm. SAVED was bitten again under water and found under water by his father, still in the crocodile's mouth. His father plunged his arm down the crocodile's mouth, opening its jaws and enabling SALVOR to free SAVED and pull him to the surface. SALVOR, with one hand round SAVED's waist, pulled him to the nearest canoe and threw him in it. Meanwhile, SAVED's father was taken under water by the crocodile and whirled round, having his arm snapped off at the elbow before being released.

All the party were now on the surface and all determined to get out of the river. However, too many attempted to clamber aboard the nearest canoe, which capsized. SALVOR left the capsized canoe and swam 10 metres into the centre of the river and collected another canoe. He returned with this and pulled one of the party into it. A girl brought her canoe over to help and the guide lifted SAVED's father into another, enabling all to get back on board. The guide took a canoe and paddled to a sandbank, towing the capsized canoe behind. SALVOR took charge of 2 other canoes and with a foot in each followed the guide to the sandbank.

Father of SAVED was treated on the sandbank, having tourniquets and bandages applied. SALVOR and guide paddled a canoe 200 metres across the river, towing SAVED and his father in a canoe behind. A landrover was luckily found on the bank and owners drove the two to Mana Pools Airport and they were flown to Harare Hospital.

Viney, Trevor Allan, (19), Student   No Case Number

Stanhope Gold Medal 1989

Case submitted by the Royal Humane Society of Australasia

PLACE/ TIME:	Waitpinga Beach, S. Australia.
CONDITIONS:	See Summary.
SALVOR:	Trevor Allan VINEY (19) Student
ATTEMPTED SAVED:	Matthew Hamilton FOYLE (27) Draughtsman DECEASED
SUMMARY:	Shortly after sunset, SALVOR was surfing his board about 200 metres from shore. His friend was on his board about 50 metres away. Conditions at the time were calm with waves of approximately 1 metre and there was still a little light.

SALVOR was sitting on his surfboard when he saw his friend splash into the water and go under for several seconds. His friend then broke the surface and shouted: "Shark - there's a shark." SALVOR immediately started to paddle towards his friend and halfway there saw the white underside of a shark's head about 50cms across. When he reached his friend, who was struggling and going up and down in the water, he could see that the shark, just under the water, still had hold of his friend's thigh. He slipped off his board and started kicking at the shark, feeling the shark's rough skin as he did so. When he sensed that the shark was driven away, SALVOR then got his friend, now stiff and shaking with shock, onto his board, managed to catch a wave and, holding and encouraging his friend on the board, swam him in until 20 metres from shore others came to help.

His badly-mauled friend failed to respond to resuscitation attempts.

As an experienced surfer, SALVOR knew well the immediate danger to which he was subjected during his rescue. As he paddled to his friend, he saw the shark beneath him and he could see the shark's jaws wrenching at his friend's thigh in the blood-filled water. He nevertheless left the comparative safety of his board to enter the water and kick the shark until it was driven away. He put his friend on the surfboard and with blood still streaming from the severed artery, swam 200m to shore in the space of five minutes, when he was completely vulnerable to attack from the same shark or other sharks attracted by the smell of blood.

Viney also awarded the Clarke Medal in Gold of the RHS of Australasia, although this was purely a symbolic award and not actually presented.

Walsh, Elaine, Housewife   No Case Number

Stanhope Gold Medal 1990

Case submitted by Liverpool Shipwreck & Humane Society

PLACE/ TIME:	Brodick Road, Shadsworth, Blackburn. 2nd December, 1989. 1600 hrs.
CONDITIONS:	House Fire.
SALVOR:	Mrs. Elaine WALSH Housewife
SAVED:	A Man
SUMMARY:	The Walsh family were approaching their home when they saw flames at the front window of a neighbour's house. As soon as they saw the extent of the flames within the front room, WALSH said he would call the fire brigade and left SALVOR on the front path with a baby in her arms and her six year old son beside her.

SALVOR heard a sound of someone moaning inside the house, so she gave her son the baby to hold and told him to go out of the garden. She pushed open the front door to find the hall full of thick smoke. She heard moaning and made her way to the living room and pushed the door open. Here she was confronted by a dense wall of smoke and terrific heat, the room was well alight with flames covering two walls. Then she saw the retired occupant of the house on his knees by the settee. He appeared to have crawled to this position and been unable to go any further. His hair was burnt and the back of his trousers had been burnt and melted onto his legs.

Despite the man's unconsciousness and dead-weight, SALVOR entered the intense heat of the room and dragged him by his hands out into the hall and then into the garden. The whole rescue took only one or two minutes at most.

WALSH returned at that moment. The rescued man came round in the fresh air and started muttering about his 22 year old son being in the house, so WALSH went to the front door to search but was prevented from entering by the smoke and intense heat which had developed. However, the fire brigade arrived shortly after and rescued the son from a veranda at the rear of the house.

Both rescued men were taken to hospital, the son being released after treatment for smoke inhalation. The father was detained for 10 weeks for extensive skin grafts.

Walsh also awarded the Bronze Fire Medal of the LSHS.

Moore, Lesley Allison, (25), Woman Police Constable   Case 81506

Stanhope Gold Medal 1991

Case submitted by the Royal Humane Society

PLACE/ TIME:	Bury Street, London SW 1.
	16th January, 1990. 11.52 hrs.
CONDITIONS:	See Summary.
ATTEMPTING SALVOR:	Woman Police Constable Lesley Allison MOORE (25) Metropolitan Police
ATTEMPTED SAVED:	Gary Westlake (-) Workman
SUMMARY:	Incident occurred when A/SAVED was erecting a protective corrugated iron roof to the scaffolding frame. This frame was 25 feet above actual roof of building. A/SAVED fell on a sheet of metal not properly attached and fell onto the sloping roof of the building, ending up on the flat roof of a 4th floor dormer window. There was no safe means to approach him, so emergency services were called. Police ambulance arrived crewed by MOORE and another PC. They were taken to the roof and shown A./SAVED two floors below. The PC went to summon assistance.

MOORE went to a flat on the 5th floor, climbed out of the dormer window in the kitchen, i.e. she was still on floor above A/SAVED. Dormer windows in these flats are not directly above one other and she therefore had to traverse a precipitous and dangerous gap which increased the difficulty of her task. There was a railing at the bottom of the sloping roof but, due to the dilapidated state of the building, it could easily have given way. MOORE sought assistance of a scaffolder who, by holding her hand, was able to swing her across the gap and enable her to jump down to top of dormer window.

In very confined conditions, MOORE gave first aid and resuscitation to A/SAVED, being restricted for space and completely unprotected. She had to turn A/SAVED over to give resuscitation and he responded when she encouraged him to breathe. MOORE removed her tunic to make a pillow and her pullover to keep him warm. The temperature was 12 degrees C and there were winds up to 43 mph. She kept up support for more than an hour.

A/SAVED could not be moved until planking and ladders were laid and had to be completed by the Fire Brigade with specialist equipment. A/SAVED did not recover.

Peters, Rodney Stephen   No Case Number

Stanhope Gold Medal 1992

Case submitted by Royal Humane Society of New South Wales

PLACE/ TIME:	Willow Tree, Bombaril Creek.
	26th January, 1991. 19.30 hrs.
CONDITIONS:	See Summary.
SALVOR:	Rodney Stephen PETERS (-) Occupation n/k
SAVED:	Neil MARTIN; Gretta MARTIN; Joshua MARTIN (9); Zachary MARTIN (6)
SUMMARY: and they	The Martin family were returning home by car. There had been heavy rain over past 2 days and 2.5 cms had fallen in the previous hour. The Martins were unaware rain had fallen and as they attempted to drive up the road they became stranded when Bombaril Creek broke its banks.

SALVOR, owner of a neighbouring property, searching for a calf in knee-deep water, noticed car lights approaching and disappearing as water went over bonnet. SALVOR had heard that more flood water was on the way and ran to warn car occupants. HE was knocked over by the force of the water but after a struggle he reached stranded SAVED. He gave a torch to Gretta MARTIN and took hold of Joshua whilst Neil MARTIN took Zachary. They started to walk but before long all were knocked over and washed back to the vehicle. SALVOR, under water, lost grip of Joshua but luckily regained his hold on finding his footing. The lights on the car had now gone out and Gretta MARTIN had lost the torch. Rain was still falling and SALVOR realised it was only a matter of time before they were hit by more water. They made another attempt through the flood, but MARTIN lost his jeans around his feet and had to be released by SALVOR. They were all knocked under water again, SALVOR holding Joshua to his chest with one hand managed to stand and return to car whilst MARTIN was also forced back with Zachary.

It was decided that one person should try to reach SALVOR's house to get a rope and MARTIN started out. When he did not return, SALVOR tied an old dog chain round Joshua and, carrying Zachary, set out once more, with Gretta hanging on to SALVOR's clothing. The force of the water made the chain cut into SALVOR's arm, so he picked him up and carried him too. Luckily they were able to make progress along flooded road and then met MARTIN and SALVOR's wife returning with an electricity cord. This was tied to a post and MARTIN made his way to his family and took his sons to safety whilst SALVOR held onto cord. Eventually SALVOR and Gretta MARTIN reached safety.

Peters also awarded the Bronze Medal of the RHS of New South Wales.

Smith, Beryl Ellen, (58), Medical Practice Manager   No Case Number

Stanhope Gold Medal 1993

Case submitted by the Royal Humane Society of Australasia

PLACE/ TIME:	Mercy Private Hospital, Melbourne.
	12th November, 1992. 12.00 hrs.
CONDITIONS:	See Summary.
SALVOR:	Beryl Ellen SMITH (58). Medical Practice Manager
SAVED:	Staff at hospital
SUMMARY:	SALVOR is employed as Business Manager of East Melbourne Radiology whose consulting suites are attached to Mercy Hospital.

Prior to the morning of 12th November, the medical and administrative staffs of several consulting suites had been harassed for more than a year by William Ernest Jolly who in 1991 had sought treatment for a broken wrist. During his treatment Jolly, who was showing signs of clinical schizophrenia, would abuse doctors treating him and also the staff, both of the suites and the hospital, firstly during visits and then by telephone, to the extent of 20 calls in one hour. Police were notified but were unable to apprehend Jolly. In the course of his harassment, he had obtained the first name 'Susan' of a specialist's secretary and towards her he developed a fixation of deep hatred.

On the night of 11/12th November, Jolly set up a campsite on a creek bank near the hospital and in the morning disguised himself with a wig, hat and glasses and strapped to his body a sawn-off .22 rifle with four magazines each of 15 rounds plus spare rounds in his pockets. He took a taxi to the hospital and after freeing the rifle, went to where he thought 'Susan' was. Enraged that she was not there, Jolly knocked to the ground the receptionist to whom he was talking and shot her in the head. He then shot her a further three times.

Jolly then began to rampage through several floors of suites shooting at glass windows and partitions, kicking at doors and screaming and swearing as patients and staff scurried for shelter. He made his way to East Melbourne Radiology where he terrorised a receptionist who fled as he fired at her. He remained in the reception area, smashing windows and firing into the ceiling.

SALVOR was alerted to the disturbance, aware that it was Jolly whom she would be confronting and, after returning to don her jacket "to look more official", walked to the reception area, joined by a male colleague and a male doctor. Convinced that the intruder was Jolly, she told the two men to stay back, fearful that their appearance might incite Jolly further. She then confronted Jolly who told her that he had shot the wrong girl upstairs and for almost 10 minutes kept talking to him to try to calm him to prevent further bloodshed while, only some metres away, another secretary was hiding behind a desk. Jolly then told her he would just shoot her (Salvor) in the leg.

SALVOR, terrified all the time she was talking to this wild uncontrolled man, then watched as he raised his rifle, took aim and fired. She reeled back against the wall but, convinced that if she fell to the wall Jolly would kill her and continue his rampage, shooting the hiding secretary and two males who were next door, managed to stay upright. She remained standing against the wall despite the pain of her wound as Jolly left. The doctor who had been with her then tried to enter but SALVOR waved him back, fearful that Jolly would return.

Police then arrived and took Jolly into custody. Described as a paranoid psychotic at his trial, he was convicted of murder and intentionally causing serious injury and sentenced to 15 years imprisonment.

Smith also awarded the Clarke Medal in Gold of the RHS of Australasia, although this was purely a symbolic award and not actually presented.

Ledden, Aaron John, (16), Student   No Case Number

Stanhope Gold Medal 1994

Case submitted by Royal Humane Society of New South Wales

PLACE/ TIME:	Hastings River Bar, Port Macquarie.
	2nd July, 1993. 12.30 hrs.
CONDITIONS:	See Summary.
SALVOR:	Aaron John LEDDEN (16) Student
A/SALVORS:	A man and a boy (16)
SAVED:	Ronald William LITTLE (retired)

SUMMARY: SALVOR (sic) was the skipper aboard his 4.9 metre half cabin runabout. Also on board were two men and SAVED's grandson (10). The runabout was returning from a fishing trip seaward off Port Macquarie when crossing the river bar it was hit by a large wave and capsized throwing everyone into the water except SAVED who was trapped in an air pocket in the cabin of the overturned boat.

SALVOR and another man were surfing nearby and immediately went to their assistance. The man placed the grandson on his back and paddled towards the shore. SALVOR went to the other two men and was told the skipper was trapped inside. He left his board with the men and dived under the water and into the boat. While he was under the water the boat was hit by more waves and SALVOR became entangled by rope and other debris floating inside the boat. He had to untangle himself before coming up for air. Meanwhile another surfer had come on the scene and given his board to the crew. He then assisted SALVOR.

The boat began to sink further into the water. There was a small cabin window partly under the water and SALVOR pulled the window and was eventually able to break it. Fish and fishing gear began rushing out. The boat began taking more water and sinking further. SALVOR put half his body through the window but couldn't see anything. He felt a person's hand and pulled hard. By placing his feet against the boat he was able to pull SAVED through.

SAVED was badly cut, weak and in shock and was assisted by SALVOR and A/SALVOR (boy 16) until the Sea Rescue boat arrived and all parties were taken on board.

Ledden also awarded the Silver Medal of the RHS of New South Wales. Certificates of Merit were presented by the RHS of New South Wales to Peter William SMITH, the surfer who had been accompanying Ledden at the time of the accident, and to Gregory Robert PORTER, the surfer who had come to their aid.

Fader, Douglas, (43), Communications Technician   No Case Number

Stanhope Gold Medal 1995

Case submitted by the Royal Canadian Humane Association

PLACE/ TIME:	Wilderness north of Fort McMurry, Alberta.
	27th August, 1993. 16.20 hrs.
CONDITIONS:	Remote wilderness area: rescue effected from crashed helicopter on fire.
SALVOR:	Douglas FADER (43) Communications Technician
SAVED:	Todd McCORMACK (28) Helicopter Pilot

SUMMARY: SAVED had picked up FADER from a remote microwave station. Shortly after take-off, the aircraft struck some cables, crashed among trees and caught fire. Fader was thrown clear but SAVED was unable to undo his seat belt due to injuries.

FADER returned to the aircraft and assisted SAVED out of the wreckage, sustaining deep third-degree burns to his face, head and arms (resulting in partial amputation of his hands and he has undergone much reconstructive surgery). He helped SAVED to a building 100 feet from the crash and called for a rescue helicopter.

Fader also awarded the Bronze Medal of the Royal Canadian Humane Association. The citation contains further details relating to the rescue:

FADER, DOUGLAS

August 27, 1993, Douglas Fader was working as a radio technician, on a microwave tower near Birch Mountain in Alberta. During the latter part of the afternoon a helicopter, piloted by Todd McCormack arrived at the scene to fly Douglas Fader back from this remote site. Following take off, when the helicopter was approximately 25 meters in the air, the helicopter rotors clipped a number of microwave guy lines. The pilot lost control and the helicopter spun into the bush spraying fuel from ruptured fuel lines. Upon impact Douglas Fader was thrown from the aircraft which immediately burst into flames. The pilot was trapped inside and due to his injuries was unable to release his seatbelt and escape the inferno. Without any thought for his personal safety Douglas Fader scrambled back into the furiously burning helicopter, released the pilot and pulled him to safety. While doing so, Douglas Fader displayed fearless courage as he received third degree burns to the face, torso, and arms in his struggle to extricate the pilot. It took some fully thirty minutes after the accident for Douglas Fader to find his way back to the site buildings to telephone for help. A helicopter was quickly dispatched from Ft. McMurray with two paramedics to recover the seriously injured men. Extensive follow-up care was required as the pilot had suffered third degree burns, broken ribs, and two broken arms, while Douglas Fader has sustained life-threatening severe burn injuries as a result of his rescue efforts.

For his fearless efforts in the face of grave danger, Douglas Fader is awarded the Bronze Medal of the Royal Canadian Humane Association.

Fader also awarded the Cross of Valour (Canada).

Boughton, Ian Maurice, Senior Constable, NSW Police Service   No Case Number

Stanhope Gold Medal 1996

Case submitted by the Royal Humane Society of New South Wales

PLACE/ TIME:	Port Waratah, New South Wales. 20th April, 1995. O815 hrs.
CONDITIONS:	Attempted rescue of a professional diver trapped in an underwater inlet cooling pipe. Salvor had no previous diving experience but decided to use the full equipment (wetsuit, boots, airline and facemask).
ATTEMPTING/SALVOR:	Senior Constable NSW Police Service Ian Maurice BOUGHTON
ATTEMPTED/SAVED:	Stephen LAMB (35) Deceased
SUMMARY:	During routine maintenance on a saltwater intake pipe of a Pumphouse, A/SAVED fully equipped and with a security line entered the inlet pipe. Two other divers, A & B, were monitoring him from the surface.

After about 5 minutes, the line pulled tight. (It was later found that A/SAVED had been sucked feet first into the intake pipe, about 3 metres below the surface and had become jammed against a mesh grill).

Pumps were shut down and the divers called for assistance. Diver A entered the water, found the mouth of the intake pipe and retrieved about 1 metre of dive hose. On a second attempt, he retrieved A/SAVED's harness, which incorporated an emergency air bottle and a face mask. A/SAVED at this stage had no air supply. Diver A left the water: B took his place and attempted to find A/SAVED, but he was unsuccessful.

BOUGHTON arrived and decided to use the airline equipment himself, even though he had no diving experience. He descended to the river bed and found the lip of the pipe, which was nominally 1 metre in diameter but was reduced to 60 cm due to crustacean growth. He entered the pipe, and climbed to a bend where visibility reduced to a few centimetres. He then went along the horizontal pipe through very murky water and found A/SAVED's open hand.

BOUGHTON tugged several times, freed A/SAVED and dragged him through the pipe to the river bed, where they became temporarily jammed under the lip of the pipe. After a short struggle, BOUGHTON was able to surface and fix a rope around A/SAVED who was lifted from the water unconscious.

A/SAVED initially responded to resuscitation by paramedics but remained in a critical condition in hospital till 2315 hrs. on 21st April, when he died.

Boughton also awarded the Silver Medal and Galleghan Award of the RHS of New South Wales.

Day, Anthony Shane, (17), Chef   No Case Number

Stanhope Gold Medal 1997

Case submitted by the Royal Humane Society of Australasia

PLACE/ TIME:	Pix Road, Davoren Park, South Australia.
	7th July 1997. 08.00 hrs.
CONDITIONS:	House fire.
SA.LVOR:	Anthony Shane DAY (17) Chef
SAVED:	Soraya YARDLEY (5)
	Joshua YARDLEY (4)
	Natasha YARDLEY (2)
SUMMARY:	DAY heard a woman screaming from across the road and saw that her house was on fire.

He ran to the woman, who was crying out for her three children still in the house. He could hear the children screaming from within the house.

With thick black smoke billowing through the front door, DAY ran into the house where he was forced to his hands and knees by the suffocating smoke, and began crawling around the lounge room yelling for the children as he went. He eventually found SORAYA huddled in a corner, picked her up, ran out through the front door and put her on the lawn near her mother. He immediately re-entered the burning house and, again crawling on the floor, found JOSHUA under the lounge room window and carried him to safety.

Fearing that the third child was still in the house, he then ran to the back of the house and saw two other men rescuing her.

All were taken to hospital and treated for smoke inhalation, burns, cuts and bruises. The house was destroyed by the fire.

Day also awarded the Clarke Medal in Silver of the RHSA, although this was purely a symbolic award and not actually presented.

Standerwick, Ian Peter, Police Constable   Case 83,443

Stanhope Gold Medal 1998

Case submitted by the Royal Humane Society

PLACE/ TIME:	Clifton Suspension Bridge, Bristol.
	8th September, 1997. 13.30hrs.
CONDITIONS:	Clifton Suspension Bridge across Avon Gorge, 200 feet above the road protection canopy.
SALVOR:	Police Constable Ian Peter STANDERWICK (-) Avon & Somerset Police
ATTEMPTED SAVED:	Miss Sally Jane WEBBER (37)
SUMMARY:	STANDERWICK and another police officer responded to an emergency call. SAVED was standing, swaying alarmingly backwards and forwards as in a trance, on a 1 foot ledge on the outside, i.e. front face, of the support tower of the Suspension bridge, overhanging the gorge.

STANDERWICK climbed over the wall onto the side and approached cautiously. As he rounded the corner he was about 4 feet from SAVED. She began falling forwards and STANDERWICK had to lunge to catch her shoulder and force her back against the wall. In doing so, he lost his balance and just managed to steady himself with the only handhold available, the flat but rough surface of the stonework.

The other officer, having approached along the main parapet, was now directly above where SAVED was standing. In his statement he says: 'I heard STANDERWICK shout "Steve - grab me!" I looked over the edge and saw him balancing on one leg. I immediately jumped onto the wall (i.e. lying prone on his stomach across the wall) and grabbed PC STANDERWICK's arm, pulling him towards me. I then grabbed the female and pulled her against the wall. She did not resist or struggle. If she had, she would have pulled PC STANDERWICK and myself over the edge.'

This same officer then had to climb over the wall onto an 18 inch ledge slightly above STANDERWICK's so that they could both drag SAVED, who was making no effort to help herself, over the wall to safety.

SAVED was taken into custody.

SPECIAL FACTORS: Neither SALVOR had a harness and there was nothing to get hold of; the only restraint was
friction between a free hand and the rough but flat stonework. Throughout the rescue, they were one
step or slip away from a vertical drop of 200 feet.

PC Standerwick was originally awarded the bronze medal of the RHS in November 1997. Following a visit to the scene of the rescue by the Secretary of the Society, his case was reviewed and his award upgraded to the silver medal in October 1998. PC Standerwick was allowed to retain his bronze award and, with the presentation of the Stanhope Gold Medal, attained the unique status of having received with all three of the Society's medallic awards then available for the same rescue.

The Assistant Salvor was PC Steven Francis DATE. He was initially awarded a Vellum Certificate in 1997, this being upgraded to a Bronze Medal in 1998.

Bailey, Vanesa, (18), student   No Case Number

Stanhope Gold Medal 1999

Case submitted by the Royal Canadian Humane Association

PLACE/ TIME: On the Beach at Pulau Pangkor, Malaysia.
                         19th January,1999. 14.00hrs.
CONDITIONS: Sea, rapidly rising and strong cross current between the beach and a small island immediately
                         offshore. Rescues effected/attempted 100-130 metres from the beach.
SALVOR: Vanessa BAILEY (18) Student
ATTEMPTED SAVED: Three SAVED, one ATTEMPTED SAVED
SUMMARY: A group of eight local Malaysia/Chinese vacationers were caught in the current, lost their
footing and were in danger of being swept away out to sea. They were poor or non-swimmers.

Immediately the alarm was given, three people entered the sea to assist. Two of these, separately, brought to safety the group of four closest to shore.

BAILEY was the first to reach the furthermost group of four, about 100-130 metres out. She took hold of a woman who seemed to be in the greatest distress and began to tow her by her clothes towards the shore. The victim was panic stricken and struggled violently so BAILEY switched her hold to a head carry and was able to complete the rescue, handing her to others who had waded out to meet them.

BAILEY immediately returned to the task and reached an unconscious man, who she towed to shore by a head carry. Once more she returned to find that both the remaining men had slipped below the surface. She dived down, grasping one of them some six feet under water; she brought him to the surface and delivered him to the shore, again using a head carry.

Yet again BAILEY, on hearing there was still one man missing, re-entered the sea and searched the area in response to shouted instructions from the shore, only to discover not a body but a log. Still she persevered, searching underwater but could not find him.

In all, BAILEY swam 500 metres, towed victims 300 metres and carried out underwater searches for a total of about 50 minutes. Following hospital treatment, all three of the victims rescued by BAILEY recovered, as did the four rescued by others. The eighth was tragically lost.

BAILEY holds the Bronze Medallion of the Life Saving Society (Canada), taken in 1995 with the Alberta and Northwest Territories Branch; she subsequently gained the Bronze Cross. She hopes to become a Lifeguard and, after University, a nurse.

Bailey also awarded the Bronze Medal of the Royal Canadian Humane Association.

Calnan, David, (45), Landscape Contractor   No Case Number

Stanhope Gold Medal 2000

Case submitted by the Royal Canadian Humane Association

PLACE/ TIME:	Tent City (a private camping ground), Dawson City, Yukon Territory. 9th July, 2000. 11.00hrs.
CONDITIONS:	Attack by a grizzly bear.
SALVOR:	David CALNAN (45) Local landscape Gardener
SAVED:	Carrie Fair (19) Municipal Pool Lifeguard

SUMMARY: Kristen TEUNISSEN (23) and Carrie FAIR were standing outside their tent when Carrie noticed a black bear about 40 feet away. They began to yell, and Kristen, who was suffering from a sprained ankle, Banged her crutches together.

The bear backed off momentarily but soon returned and came very close to Carrie. At this point, she dropped to her hands and knees and was bitten by the bear on her thigh. Kristen poked the bear with her crutches and it briefly left, but it returned and continued to bite. Kristen felt that she was unable to deal with the situation due to her physical ailment and ran to a road about 70 yards away to summon help. While she was gone, the bear continued to maul Carrie.

Davis CALNAN was working nearby and heard Kristen's cries for help.. He immediately grabbed a pickaxe and ran up the hill to find Carrie with the bear on top of her, eating her left leg. He first picked up a stick and threw it at the bear, which resulted in the bear charging towards him, then stopping and returning to maul Carrie. He was afraid to use the pickaxe for fear that he would strike Carrie.

The bear then took Carrie by the back of the neck and dragged her a short distance to the woods. CALNAN grabbed another log and threw it at the bear. The bear once again stopped its attack and briefly charged CALNAN, only to return to Carrie and again grabbed her by the head and dragged her further into the woods.

Out of desperation, CALNAN then grabbed a 4 foot long log, ran up to the bear and hit it several times. This resulted in driving the bear a safe distance away. CALNAN stayed with Carrie while the bear circled them from a distance.

The Dawson City Royal Canadian Mounted Police and the Yukon Conservation Officers, who had been contacted, then arrived on the scene.

Carrie was taken by ambulance to Dawson City Nursing Station and treated briefly before being rushed by aircraft to Vancouver. She has undergone multiple surgeries in an attempt to save her leg, the calf of which was almost completely eaten away. She is now able to walk with a leg brace.

Calnan also awarded the Bronze Medal of the Royal Canadian Huamane Association.

R.H.S. POLICE MEDAL

2000

The Royal Humane Society
Police Medal

1　INTRODUCTION

At a Committee Meeting of the Royal Humane Society held on 8 August 2000, it was resolved that there should be a new medal in silver gilt, given annually for the case of the greatest gallantry by a Police Officer of the United Kingdom, during the year.

2　ELIGIBILITY

Cases eligible are those adjudicated on by the Committee between 1st September of the preceding year and 31st August of the current year. The best case will be determined from all categories of award, at the discretion of the Committee.

(The timing is in phase with but separate from the award of the Stanhope Gold Medal. If a Police Officer wins the Stanhope, the Police Medal will be given to the next best Police case).

3　COMMITTEE

The Committee will make its decision on the Police Medal at the January Meeting each year.

4　PRESENTATION

The medal will be presented at the Annual General Court in London in May, or as arranged with the Chief Constable.

Maj. Gen. C. Tyler CB
Secretary
23rd Nov. 2000

(It should be noted that whilst police officers who are awarded the Stanhope Gold Medal are not eligible also to receive the Police Medal, officers may nevertheless receive and wear the Police Medal in addition to RHS Silver or Bronze Medals awarded for the same rescue. The ribbon of the Police Medal is coloured blue-yellow-blue in equal parts.)

Martin, Wayne Alexander, (34), Police Constable   Case 83,842

Police Medal 2000

PLACE/ TIME:	A507 Ampthill to Ridgmont road, Bedfordshire.
	16th March, 1999. 16.50hrs.
CONDITIONS:	A two-vehicle fatal RTA with fire.
SALVOR:	Police Constable Wayne Alexander MARTIN (34) Bedfordshire Police
ATTEMPTED SAVED:	Name withheld DECEASED 16th March 1999
SUMMARY:	MARTIN and another officer were sent to the reported accident, where they found one of the vehicles engulfed in flames. There was also an ambulance with a crew of three standing a short distance from the burning vehicle; one gestured to MARTIN to bring a fire extinguisher from his car but this surprised him as the crashed vehicle was a mass of flames.

When MARTIN reached it, he found that the driver's door was open and he was shocked to see a woman (A/SAVED) in the driver's seat, with no one trying to get her out. She was conscious but groaning and leaning to one side; her legs were engulfed in flames and appeared to be on fire.

MARTIN threw down the extinguisher and, ignoring the flames, grabbed A/SAVED by her shoulders and attempted to pull her from the car. His first attempt failed but he managed to get her out and drag her clear. He then called for help from the others and carried her about 20 feet away.

A/SAVED's clothing was burnt from the waist down and her legs were in fact on fire; one of the ambulance crew put a wet blanket over them. At this juncture the car exploded.

R.H.S. SILVER MEDALS

1951 to 2000

MacFarlane, Alexander, (46) Ship's Engineer Case 62285

At 10 p.m. on 10th October, 1951, it being very dark, salvor and saved were boarding a fishing vessel alongside the quay, Stornoway, Isle of Lewis, Scotland, when Mr Murdoch Macleod, who was injured in the war and has an artificial limb, was overcome by giddiness followed by illness making it not possible for him to control his actions or account for them. He fell into the harbour between ship and quay. Without hesitation Mr MacFarlane went in after Mr Macleod, although he knew that there was danger of being crushed between the ship and quay or being trapped under the bilge-keel on going in. The illness of Mr Macleod made him a difficult subject to control. None the less Mr MacFarlane supported and controlled Mr Macleod for 30 minutes in dangerous circumstances until a rescue party hauled both up.

Pancras Eddy, (32), Supervisor, Sarawak Co-operative Development Department Case 62388

In a river, Tanjong Gelagah, Ulu Layar, Betong, Sarawak. At 5.30 p.m. on 27th March, 1951, Mr Eddy was travelling with twenty others in a covered boat fitted with an outboard engine across the river. The river is here 60 yards wide and 15 feet deep at low tide ; the current at the time of the accident was running at a speed of five knots. The engine caught fire and the fire spread to some petrol in a can inboard. Mr Eddy, caught between two fires, forced his way through the side of the boat and dived into the river. While swimming ashore he heard the screams of a woman (Yak Anak Bundan) who was trapped in the burning boat. Mr Eddy at once turned and swam back to the boat which he re-entered through the hole he had made to effect his exit. He found the woman with her clothes on fire. Ignoring the danger he grasped her, got her through the hole in the boat's side and into the water. With great difficulty, owing to the current, he swam 30 yards with her to the shore and brought her to safety. The woman died two days later. Mr Eddy sustained burns on his right hand in effecting the rescue.

Somiah, Samuel Bulleh, (35), Timber Merchant Case 62428
Williams, Joseph Samuel

Gold Coast, West Africa at 6.45 p.m. it then being very dark with no visibility and torrential rain beating down, the Ankobra River Mouth Ferry was making its last trip of the day. The river is 170 yards wide, 50 feet deep and the current is very strong. The ferry consists of pontoons, cable drawn and actuated by a hand operated winch, the crew being one headman and six labourers. The cargo for the trip was two five-ton lorries and between thirty-one to thirty-three passengers.

Despite the torrential rain, the darkness and the adverse conditions, the ferry made good progress and in ten minutes it had got half-way across. A noise was then heard and it was later found that the main towing cable had parted, it being conjectured that the safety chains had broken first. The ferry swung round in the current, drifted loose and went 200 yards downstream, submerging. The lorries remained above water and people climbed on them while other passengers swam ashore. The ferry was towing a canoe, and Mr Somiah, with great difficulty, got the seven persons saved onto this. Mr Williams, who had swum ashore, now returned. He dived and with great difficulty released the canoe tow line from the ferry. He then contributed to the rescue of all. Both salvors were in the river in conditions of, great danger for over an hour. Attempts were made to rescue the remaining passengers and crew without avail and only seven bodies and one hand were recovered from the sunk pontoons.

Milner, Peter Frank Morrell, Lieutenant, R.N. Case 62441

In the sea, Umhloti Beach, Durban, South Africa. At 4 p.m. on 16th February, 1952, Mr Neaves and Mr Brook were seen to be in difficulties on the beach. The wind was blowing at a rate of 11-16 miles per hour, there was a moderate swell, breakers 10-30 feet high were coming over the rocks and the tide was rising. The beach consists of a pool guarded by two wings of off-lying rocks and it is possible to walk waist-deep from the wings of the rocks to the beach proper. In the centre, however, there is a deep water channel through which big seas were coming in. The two men had got onto the rocks and decided to surf back to the beach from the centre gap. They were seen to be in difficulties, having been swimming against a very strong current for half an hour.

Lieutenant Milner and another Naval Officer swam out. They saw Mr Neaves, who was the stronger swimmer, haul Mr Brooks onto the rocks. Lieutenant Milner got onto the rocks and waded round the wing; his companion swam back. Messrs Neaves and Brook again attempted to reach the shore but were separated by an extra large wave, and Mr Neaves was seen to be in danger. Lieutenant Milner then went in with an inflated rubber tube, reached Mr Neaves and escorted him in with Mr Neaves holding the tube.

Meanwhile the sea had carried Mr Brook out beyond the rocks. He showed no sign of life and had been in the water for 45 minutes, so an immediate rescue was essential. A line arrived and Lieutenant Milner with two others went out with it, those on shore forming a chain to make it reach as far as possible. It was not, however, long enough and Lieutenant Milner, with complete disregard for his own safety, let go and swam to the rocks. Waves 10 - 320 feet high were pounding over them but Lieutenant Milner struggled to the seaward side, being knocked over and injured in doing so. The same wave brought in Mr Brook and pounded him on the rock. It was then possible for the line to be secured and Mr Brook hauled in. Lieutenant Milner was badly grazed on feet, legs, chest, back, arms and hands and sustained a deep cut over the eye necessitating three stitches.

Mr Brook did not respond to artificial respiration. His body was recovered from a distance of 200 yards out by a salvor.

Lewanavanua, Marika Ului, (29), School Teacher   Case 63589

Saved Luisa Tinaikaboa, female aged 60-70 at Nakoronawa, Nakasaleka, Kadavu, Fiji, in a tidal wave following an earthquake.

On 14th September, 1953, a tidal wave, resulting from an earthquake, struck the village, knocking down 40 houses. The wave surged inland at a height of 8-10 feet. People ran for high ground calling that an old woman was still in one of the top houses of the village. The time was shortly after mid-day.

On hearing the call Lewanavanua ran from the School to look for the woman. He leapt on top of one of the houses which was floating on the tidal wave and saw the other houses being swept past him.

Undeterred by the general chaos Lewanavanua kept his head and, looking about him, saw a woman's clothing floating in the fast-moving current. He dived into the raging waters among the houses being swept away and, with great difficulty, found the woman half submerged. He secured her and dragged her to the shore.

She was unconscious on being saved and salvor applied artificial respiration to restore her to unconsciousness

Sayer, Robert William, (21), Leading Seaman, Royal Navy   Case 63847

In the Inner Harbour, Singapore, during diving operations, 200 yards from the shore in a depth of 20 feet. The rescue was made in shark infested waters, the man saved, who unfortunately did not recover, having been bitten by one.

Diving was in progress on 28th July, 1954, and the following is an extract from the report of the Commanding Officer, Lieutenant Commander H. Wardle, R.N.:
Sayer was a member of a diving team under my command which was employed carrying out a diving survey of the Singapore area.

At about 12.25 on 28th July, 1954, Leading Seaman Charles Brian Larkin, one of the divers who were diving at this time, surfaced about 100 feet from the diving boat. It was soon clear that he was in serious difficulty as his hands were bleeding and the water around him was extensively bloodstained.

Sayer immediately volunteered to go to Larkin's assistance and, on permission being granted, dived into the water with no thought of possible danger to himself. Sayer was closely followed into the water by Able Seaman Thomas Charles Sherris.

The action taken by Leading Seaman Sayer resulted in the rapid recovery of Leading Seaman Larkin from the water. He was lifted into a landing craft which was standing by. Sayer continued to show great initiative during Larkin's subsequent transfer to hospital.

It was unfortunate that Leading Seaman Larkin's wounds were so extensive that there was no hope of saving his life. This does not, however, reduce in any way the credit due to Leading Seaman Sayer.

Able Seaman Thomas Charles Sherris (22) was awarded the Bronze Medal.

Chrystal, Ian, Marine, Royal Marines   Case 68013

On the 26th November, 1961 three young men went climbing in the area of the Llanberis Pass, Snowdonia, North Wales. All were roped. The most experienced fell and was killed. The other two, stranded, shouted for help. Their shouts were heard by military climbers, one of whom went to get help, while the other, Marine Ian Chrystal, Royal Marines, climbed up the very dangerous main wall two-hundred and fifty feet, and calmed down the two young men. It was now pitch dark. A considerable time later Chrystal then lowered the two men in turn to an officer party which had climbed to eighty feet below.

Koso, Mathew, (31), Farmer   Case 69244

PLACE/ TIME:	From an attack by a Shark in the Sea at Susukana Santa Ysabel, British Solomon Islands Protectorate. 29 September 1963. 1pm.
CONDITIONS:	Fine weather, calm sea, attempted rescue 50 yards from shore in 8-10 feet of water. Attempting salvor swam 5 yards.
ATTEMPTING SALVOR:	Matthew KOSO (37) Farmer
SAVED:	Addison DOHI (31) Farmer
SUMMARY:	Two boys and two adults were fishing off a reef at SUSUKANA. A shark about 10 feet long

attacked DOHI, who was swimming in the water, biting him on the left thigh. KOSO swam to his aid and grasped DOHI around the chest and pulled him towards a reef so as to get him out of deep water. Before they reached the reef the Shark again attacked DOHI biting him on the right leg. However KOSI drove the shark off with a spear. The Shark circled the two men; but KOSO was able to drag DOHI onto the reef and then brought him back to the shore along the reef, a distance of about 100 yards to avoid entering deep water. DOHI unfortunately died.

Hussey, John Louis David, (25), 2nd Officer, Merchant Navy   Case 70478

PLACE/ TIME:	In the Atlantic, Latitude 41° 58' N; 09° 32' W; approximately 25 miles off the Portuguese coast. 1st January 1966. 09.58 hours.
CONDITIONS:	Westerly, gusting to gale force after prolonged period of bad weather. Weather overcast. Sea moderate. Heavy waves over a heavy swell. Currents flowing southerly at 1 to 2 knots. Vessel was rolling moderately, shipping occasional seas on weather decks. Cold. Rescue 25 miles from the Portuguese coast in 6000 feet of water. Salvor Hussey swam 200 yards in heavy seas and swell. RESUSCITATION.
SALVOR/ RESTORER:	2nd Officer John Louis David HUSSEY (25), SS *Mobil Enterprise* Merchant Navy
ASSISTANTS:	Boat crew 3rd Officer Derek Penny (24) SS *Mobil Enterprise*, (in charge) 4th Engineer Kenneth EVANS (22) SS *Mobil Enterprise* 5th Engineer Owen Magnus BENGTSON (22) SS *Mobil Enterprise* Able Seaman Abdulla MOHAMED SS *Mobil Enterprise* Able Seaman Ahmed SULLEYMAN SS *Mobil Enterprise*
SAVED/ RESTORED:	Cadet David Robert PORTER (16) Deck Cadet SS *Mobil Enterprise*
SUMMARY:	Cadets PORTER and BROOK were on deck when a chest high wave caught PORTER off

guard. He grabbed a valve and held on desperately; but the tremendous force of the water tore him loose and washed him out to sea.

BROOK raised the alarm. The helmsman immediately executed a Williamson turn. In a few minutes the ship had completely come about and the masthead lookout sighted the man overboard (PORTER) floating on his back apparently unconscious. Twice the boy PORTER was seen to disappear.

HUSSEY donned a life-jacket and disregarding the great personal danger jumped overboard and swam out to the cadet. While HUSSEY held PORTER's head above water the Captain PAWLOWICZ skilfully manouveured the *Enterprise* into a position to screen the men in the water from the buffeting seas.

In minutes, a motor lifeboat, crewed by the Assistants was on its way to the rescue battling to make headway against the heavy swells. Great difficulty was experienced in getting PORTER back onto the *Enterprise* in view of the roughness of the seas. In fact though drums of oil were poured on the water in an effort to smooth the waves, due to the rolling of the *Enterprise* the boat had eventually to be abandoned after twice nearly swamping.

Saved had been in water 27 Minutes. Limp and pale. Just breathing but losing interest and consciousness. HUSSEY made Porter vomit in the water. EVANS applied Holder Neilsen in the boat. PORTER took an hour to come around.

Bonnett, Nigel Leonard, (15), Schoolboy   Case 71804

PLACE/ TIME: From an attack by a leopard in Nairobi National Park, Nairobi, Kenya, East Africa. 19th March,   1967 (Case received 13th July 1968). 2.15 pm.
CONDITIONS: See Summary. A roused leopard is said by experts in evidence to attack with indescribable fury as   happened in this case.
SALVOR: Nigel Leonard BONNETT (15) Schoolboy.
ASSISTANT: Miss Elizabeth Margaret GILES. Did not leave her vehicle.
SAVED: Leonard Harry BONNETT (44) Technical Manager.
SUMMARY: Mr Harry BONNETT, Honorary Warden of Nairobi Game Park was releasing a leopard in the Forest area. The release mechanism of the leopard cage jammed. Harry BONNETT went to free the mechanism and having done so was returning to the cab of his vehicle, when the leopard got his claw in the small space that resulted after the obstruction had been cleared, forced open the door and leapt right onto BONNETT very badly mauling him.

Harry BONNETT's son Nigel seeing his father's predicament leapt out of the cab and ran to his father's aid. The leopard then turned on him and mauled him as well. Eye witnesses' daughter in second car sizing up situation, drove the car towards the leopard. This scared the leopard, who jumped off its victims and ran off into the forest. Mr. Harry BONNETT incidentally had previous to this accident released many leopards using the self same cage without incident. Salvor suffered deep clawing on either side of head and bite to left hand. The father, 125 stitches in face and hand.

Testimonial on Vellum voted to Elizabeth Giles.

Ranabaca, Ivamere, (41), Housewife   Case 73954

PLACE/ TIME: From a wild boar at Nauruuru Farm, Natewa, Fiji. 15th September, 1971. Time not stated.
CONDITIONS: See Summary.
SALVOR: Miss Ivamere RANABACA (41) Housewife.
SAVED: Mrs. Arieta TARAI, Housewife.
SUMMARY: A Villager, Uraia TARAI, was attacked and fatally wounded by a wild boar. The boar then went for SAVED (his wife) who ran away, the boar following her.

Salvor arrived on the scene and shouted and the boar turned and charged her. She stood her ground and was wounded when the boar attacked her, but she jumped on its back and held its ears, "so they run round and round". She was further wounded, but held on and told SAVED to cut the boar's hind leg with a knife. This SAVED did, the boar being thus halted. SALVOR then took the knife herself and finished the boar off. The High Commissioner in forwarding the form writes:- "You will note that the Miss Ranabaca is the daughter of the deceased, but we consider that this has been an exceptional case of bravery and hope that the Committee will consider that these special circumstances may justify an exception being made".

Pese, Meleane, (23), Meteorological Observer   Case 74446

PLACE/ TIME: From swirling seas caused by a hurricane at Funafuti, Ellice Islands. 21st October 1972. 10.15   pm.
CONDITIONS: See Summary. Governor states disaster conditions. 40 feet wave. Winds up to 150 mph.
SALVOR: Miss Meleane PESE (23) Observer, Meteorological Station Funafuti.
SAVED: Salai PEIFANGA (7).
                        Mrs Manaema PEIFANGA (about 45) Housewife.
SUMMARY: Hurricane "Bebe" hit the Meteorological station and destroyed it. Two people were killed and Miss PESE was hurled outside by the force of the water and knocked senseless. (Her face was heavily bruised for several weeks afterwards). Miss PESE came to in the swirling sea and rubble and while struggling to keep above water, she saw the seven year old little girl. She got the child onto her back and swam to a palm tree to which she clung.

Shortly afterwards she made contact with the child's mother, whose six-month old grandchild had been washed out of her arms and who was in a very distraught state. She persuaded the woman to swim to the palm tree and calmed her sufficiently to cling to it. PESE supported the child on her back and ensured that the woman clung to the tree for a period of about five hours through the night, by which time the water had subsided sufficiently for them all to make their way to safety. In the Governor's report he stresses that he considers it improbable in the conditions prevailing, that the child could have survived had not PESE supported her throughout the night and also it is quite likely that the woman in her distraught and panic-stricken state would have succumbed too if PESE had not been there to take control of her.

Besley, David, (17), Market Gardener — Case 74582

PLACE/ TIME:	From danger of explosion, falling debris or collapse of aircraft wreckage after the air crash at Basle, Switzerland. 10th April, 1973. 9.50 am.
CONDITIONS:	See Summary.
SALVOR:	David BESLEY (17) Market Gardener
SAVED:	Mrs BESLEY, Housewife
	Mrs Jennifer BOWEN, Housewife
	Jonathan BOWEN (11) Schoolboy
	An Air Hostess
SUMMARY:	The plane crashed and broke into three sections, in a wooded area during a snow storm. BESLEY was knocked unconscious; but came to.

Though injured himself; BESLEY moved twisted seats and released his mother and lifted her clear of the plane. He returned to the plane and released from the wreckage a woman and her eleven year old son. He again returned to the plane and helped a badly hurt air hostess to get clear. Once more he went back to the plane and made others, who were trapped by tangled metal, as comfortable as possible.

BESLEY then walked with another man a considerable distance to obtain local help. Honorary Representative points out very real risks from explosion, falling debris and collapse of aircraft wreckage. Honorary Representative has also checked with Home Office, Department of Trade and Industry, Ministry of Civil Aviation and Foreign and Commonwealth Office that they are happy about this case going forward to the Royal Humane Society.

Fakalelu, Viliami Malolo, (22), Constable, Eua Police   **Posthumous Award**   Case 74871

PLACE/ TIME:	Mafanua Harbour, Eua, Tonga.
	19th June, 1973. 10.45am
CONDITIONS:	Exceptionally high freak seas near the harbour entrance swept an inter-island steamer with 55 passengers on to a coral reef. Ship sank, many passengers thrown into boiling sea. High wind, blustery weather, very cold sea, high tide, strong currents.
	<u>RESCUSCITATION</u>
	Distance swum 2 _ times 160 yards, in 18 feet of water.
SALVOR:	Police Constable Viliami Malolo FAKALELU (22) Eua Police (DECEASED)
RESTORER:	Asppeli VAILEA (no details)
SAVED/RESTORED:	Ana KALIPA (31) Housewife
	Mele KOLOSITI (56) Housewife
SUMMARY:	FAKALELU swam twice to the stricken ship in unbelievable conditions. Each time he brought back one woman but on his third attempt he disappeared. The Police report states that it mist have required super-human effort and a tremendous amount of courage.

The Minister of Police of Tonga states that FAKALELU went far beyond the normal call of duty and that his actions are worthy of the highest praise and reflect the greatest credit upon the Department as a whole.

The younger of the two women was apparently lifeless when brought ashore. Artificial respiration (Expelled air) was applied by VAILEA for eight minutes after which breathing re-commenced.

Resuscitation Certificate voted to Vailea.

Porter, Kenneth James, (29), Boilermaker Case 75151

PLACE/ TIME:	A tall chimney stack in Woolwich Dock Yard, SE 18.
	18th May, 1974. 11.50am.
CONDITIONS:	Top of chimney 167 feet above ground, See summary.
SALVORS:	Kenneth James PORTER (29) Boilermaker
	Acting Sub-Officer John Patrick McCABE (26) London Fire Brigade
	Fireman Sydney James LANE (29) London Fire Brigade
	Fireman Brian Leonard CUFFE (23) London Fire Brigade
SAVED:	Harry WALKER Foreman Steeplejack
SUMMARY:	SAVED and two steeplejacks were on the top of the Chimney, which was being demolished. SAVED was levering a segment of masonry off the top, when it pivoted, pinning him down and severely injuring him.

This was, of course, seen from below, and the Fire Brigade were called. PORTER, who had recently taken a first aid course, decided to go to the top to render first aid. The ladder consisted of 10-foot lengths of wooden ladder, joined together with metal sleeves and attached to the Chimney every 20 feet by cords. Thus there was a good deal of movement when the ladder was being climbed. The ladder ended three feet short of the top of the stack, and climbers had to find hand-holds on the brickwork. The top itself was 22 inches wide.

PORTER successfully negotiated this climb, and examined SAVED, who was found to have internal injuries.
The Fire Brigade arrived and McCAGE, LANE and CUFFE, climbed the ladder with a walkie-talkie, ladder etc. Meanwhile the Police, recollecting that there was an air display at Biggin Hill, 'phoned there, and a RN Helicopter was despatched. This was as well, as the Fire Brigade were of the opinion that, with the limited equipment which could be used on the Chimney top, it would have taken a matter of hours to get the man down. They therefore tied the man to themselves (as he was becoming delirious and agitated) until the Helicopter arrived and took him off. Both the Police Report and that of the Divisional Fire Officer consider the hazard to all involved was quite exceptional. Unfortunately SAVED died a fortnight later - SALVORS were commended by the Coroner.

The three Firemen were recommended for the Queen's Commendation for Brave Conduct.

Britten, Brian, (33), Builder Case 75177

PLACE/ TIME:	From a high cliff at Daddyhole Plain, Torquay.
	19th July ,1974. 6.45 pm.
CONDITIONS:	Cliff about 175 feet high.
SALVOR:	Brian BRITTEN (33) Builder
SAVED:	Andrew William PALMER (11) Schoolboy
SUMMARY:	SAVED, going to fetch a football, fell about 25 feet into a gully. BRITTEN went to his aid. To do this he had to jump onto a pinnacle 6 feet below, and 3 feet out from the cliff face, about 12 to 18 inches across and with a sheer 150 foot drop on the seaward side. Thence he made his way to the boy and tended him for some minutes until the Rescue Services arrived.

Gibson, Thomas Alexander Edwin, (52), Retired Army Officer Case 75652

PLACE/ TIME:	The Railway Line at Reading Railway Station
	2nd March, 1973. 4.40pm.
CONDITIONS:	See Summary
SALVOR:	Major Thomas Alexander Edwin GIBSON (52) Retired Army Officer
SAVED:	Miss Fiona Clare McCAFFEREY (26) Unemployed
SUMMARY:	As the Birmingham train was pulling in, SAVED threw her self onto the line. She was about 40 yards from the train, which was then doing 20 mph., she was lying across the lines. GIBSON jumped down and attempted to pull her clear, but finding he could not, got her lengthways between the tracks, himself rolling clear onto the ballast beside the track as the train came on them. As he did so, he saw that she had got her leg over the line and he just had time to put it back. The train came to a rest with her under the third coach, virtually unharmed. (This was her third attempt at Reading Station). Late submission of Case explained by Hon. Representative is due to administrative error.

Parsons, John Valentine, (40), Court Security Officer   Case 75924

PLACE/ TIME: Penge East Southern Region Railway Station. (Northbound Platform)
                15th October, 1975. (Lateness due to having been put up for a Sovereign's award and turned down). 7.55 am.
CONDITIONS: See Summary
SALVOR: John Valentine PARSONS (40) A Security Officer at the Old Bailey Central Criminal Court
SAVED: Miss Maureen JONES (20) a Printer (She suffers from fits but they are normally of a mild nature)
SUMMARY: The saved twenty year old girl was reading a newspaper. She dropped the paper and on bending down suffered an epileptic fit. The platform was crowded and no-one went to her aid except PARSONS, who saw what had happened as he came through the ticket barrier. He ran forty yards down the platform, jumped onto the railway line as a train was approaching the Station some forty yards away. He reached the girl who was lying face-down on the rail. PARSONS tried to stop the train by putting up his hand. He then tried to lift the girl onto the platform; but she was too heavy. He then very quickly pushed her backwards so she was in the alcove between the platform wall and the railway line. As he did this the girl struggled. Seeing the train was nearly upon them, PARSONS attempted to jump onto the platform. He got most of his body on the platform; but his left leg was struck by the train. The saved girl moved and was also struck by the train. Both Salvor and Saved were taken to hospital. Parsons was treated for cuts and bruises. The girl suffered a fractured spine and injuries to the head and arms; but she is expected to make a full recovery.

Parsons was initially awarded the RHS Bronze Medal, but this was subsequently upgraded.

Blackburn, Leonard John, (46), Company Director   Case 76222

PLACE/ TIME: From a high Chimney Stack at Blackburn Suspended Scaffolding, Low Wells Works, Briggate, Shipley, Yorks.
                22nd Aug., 1976. 12.30 am.
CONDITIONS: Chimney 105 feet high.
SALVORS: Leonard John BLACKBURN (46) Company Director
                Chief Inspector Samuel David SOWDEN (37) West Yorkshire Metropolitan Police
SAVED: David GREEN (22) Labourer
SUMMARY: A man was seen on the roof of a building by a night watchman, and when challenged he climbed up the jack ladder to the top of the Chimney. Police and a turntable ladder were sent for, and SOWDEN went up on the turntable ladder.
He found SAVED lying across the rim of the Chimney (which was only about 1 foot broad), he had lost his nerve and was sobbing and moving about. The ladder was 4 feet short of the top of the Chimney, so SOWDEN secured himself to a safety harness and leaned across and held the man's ankle to stop him falling. Meanwhile, unknown to the others, BLACKBURN had climbed up the jack ladder, and he and SOWDEN tied SAVED to the ladder with a rope. BLACKBURN then climbed on to the narrow rim, and with great difficulty got SAVED into the space between the jack ladder and the Chimney. After strenuous efforts the two SALVORS got him onto the turntable ladder.

During the 10 to 15 minutes of the rescue SAVED "who was drunk and had lost his nerve, was struggling, abusive and extremely uncooperative".

Bronze Medal voted to Sowden.

Rusiate Rarawa Volavola, (48), Labourer   Case 76933
Miliakere Rarogo Vesikalou, (24), Teacher

PLACE/ TIME: A reef in the sea off Waimoro Bay, Fiji.
                30th July, 1977. 3.30pm.
CONDITIONS: See Summary.
SALVORS: RUSIATE RARARAWA VOLAVOLA (48) Labourer
                MILIAKERE RAROGO VESIKALOU (24) School Teacher (Female)
                SAVIRIO VEIMOKO BOILA (43) Handyman
                SALANIETA DEDEVU (17) Student
                NEMESIO BOILA (14)

ASSISTANT SALVORS/ RESTORERS:	JONACANI RATUTINI Boatman Rescue Launch PENI NAWADVADUA Crew Rescue Launch APAKUKI RATUKOKA Crew Rescue Launch MRS. OLGA SCOTT MR. L.S. SCOTT ELESI MARAMA TAKA BOWER LOMA TAKAPE Interpreter to Mr & Mrs Scott
SAVED:	x LEONE CAMA (11) x INOKE GACEVI (7) <u>DECEASED</u> x CHARLIE MATALEI x TOM MOGEACAGI x All non-swimmers

SUMMARY: An open punt, powered by a 15 hp outboard motor and containing 3 adults and 6 children, four of them non-swimmers, left Levuka at 2pm to return to Makogai. The sea conditions were good but freshening.

At approximately 3.30pm the punt was overturned by a large wave on a reef off Waimoro Bay. All the occupants were flung into the sea. SAVIRIO helped by SALANIETA and NEMESIO managed to get the non-swimmers to the boat and eventually got it onto the reef, although the motor was lost. The boat was constantly pounded by waves and was tossed about with the children clinging to it.

Prior to the rescue one of the children, INOKE, swamped by a wave let go and drowned.

RUSIATE & MILIAKERE left SAVIRIO in charge and began to swim to the nearest landfall, Leading Point, about 3 miles from the reef at 4pm. After a long swim, at times against the tide and in the company of a shark, they reached the SCOTT's house at Nasau at 9.30pm. Both were distressed, extremely cold and shocked. RUSIATE, recently having had pneumonia, was completely exhausted and barely conscious. Mrs SCOTT attended to RUSIATE and MILIAKERE whilst Mr SCOTT went out and organised a rescue boat driven by JONACANI and crewed by PENI & APAKUKI.

The rescue boat left immediately in bright moonlight and a roughish sea and spotted the punt on the reef with the waves breaking over it. They managed to get the survivors into their boat and returned to the SCOTT's house at Nasau at about 10.30pm. They were all very cold, shocked and suffering from exposure. MOGEACAGI and NATALEI (sic) required instant attention and in particular MOGEACAGI. This was given, and indeed to all of them by Mrs SCOTT, assisted by ELESI MARAMA, TAKA BOWER & LOMA TAKAPE, the interpreter, through the night until the Medical boat arrived next day.

Testimonial on Vellum voted to Savirio, Salanieta and Nemesio.
Certificate of Commendation voted to Jonacani, Peni, Apakuki, Mrs Olga Scott, Elesi Marama, Taka Bower, Loma Takape and Mr L.S. Scott.

McKechnie, Anthony M.D.L., Captain, Royal Artillery   Case 77256

PLACE/ TIME:	An avalanche - Pazolastok, Andermatt, Switzerland 1st January 1979.
CONDITIONS:	See summary.
SALVOR:	Captain A.M.D. McKECHNIE, R.A.
SAVED:	Mark McKENZIE

SUMMARY: On the morning of 1st January 1979 a well equipped and experienced party of 6 set out on skis from Obabralpass to climb Pazolastok. The party were expected to return to Andermatt before dark.

During the ascent SALVOR and two others were caught in an avalanche. The two were freed without too much difficulty, but SALVOR was buried deeper and it took an hour to free him. The weather was then deteriorating, the temperature dropping, and the wind getting up. SALVOR, upon being freed, was found to be suffering from hyperthermia (sic), had been unconscious for an hour, and was given an additional cold weather suit to wear.

It was decided in view of the severe change in the weather, and the possibility of further avalanches to abandon the ascent, and to descend by a different route into another valley. The party were crossing another slope when they were all engulfed by a huge avalanche 1,500 metres wide and 1,500 metres long. SALVOR, flung through the snow for some time, felt the avalanche slowing down. He was able to swim towards the surface, and when the avalanche stopped his head was clear. He worked his way out, and found his skis were ripped from his boots and his gloves were missing. (His ribs had been broken and he was severely bruised). The wind by now was gale force, visibility nil and the temperature down to minus 25°C.

SALVOR set out to look for the rest of the party, finding a broken piece of one ski, and his gloves on the way. The rest of the party had been carried into another gully and although SALVOR heard their rescue beacons operating, and he attempted to dig for them with his broken ski, the vast area of the avalanche made his attempts unlikely to succeed. (They were later found widely separated).

SALVOR eventually decided, exhausted from digging search holes, to go for help. He set off, in zero visibility and deep driving snow, down the mountain on his hands and knees, using his broken ski for support.

After several hours - it was now dark - he found a mountain hut and crawled in to wait for daylight. The night was bitterly cold and, despite his broken ribs, kept himself alive by exercise. He carried on down the mountain at first light, and arriving at a village raised the alarm.

Swiss rescue teams had already been alerted by the non-return of the party the previous night, but due to the adverse weather conditions had decided no attempt could be made before dawn on the 2nd January. SALVOR within 15 minutes of arriving, and despite his injuries, was airborne in a helicopter and able to direct it, and the search parties, with sniffer dogs, to the scene. SAVED, who had been buried for over 20 hours, had by this time managed to get a hand above the snow. He was sighted and dug out. The other four climbers, who were later found, had unfortunately perished.

The President of the Combined Services Winter Sports Association in strongly recommending SALVOR for an award said "SALVOR'S determination in first of all trying to dig for his companions when injured and in the most appalling weather conditions was very brave, and his magnificent effort in crawling down the mountain to raise the alarm and then immediately directing the search party undoubtedly saved the life of SAVED."

Farrant, Roger Duncan, (24), Research Chemist   Case 77632

PLACE/ TIME:	The Sea, Canniss Buoy, off Fowey Harbour, Cornwall. 30th July 1979. 11.00 hrs.
CONDITIONS: 90	Wind S.SW Force 4. Sea 3-4 foot waves. Visibility good. Cloudy. Tide E. 1,000 yds from shore in 60- feet of water. Salvors swam 40 yards.
SALVORS:	Roger Duncan FARRANT (24) Research Chemist
	CPO James BAULD Royal Navy Diver
ASSISTANT SALVOR/ RESTORER:	Michael John CASSERLY (44) RN (Retired)
RESTORERS:	Lawrence Alwyn HARBOR Director
	John David FARRELL Designer
SAVED:	Peter Martin Bolton CROWTHER (15)
	Simon Edward CROWTHER (13)

SUMMARY: The Sail Training Vessel *Rona* was overflown by a light aircraft, which, turning downwind, lost height, ditched and overturned. *Rona* downsailed, approached the aircraft, which was vertical and sinking. The pilot and a photographer were clinging to the tail. The pilot shouted that the two boys were trapped inside. FARRANT and CASSERLY entered the water from *Rona*. FARRANT dived to the aircraft, with no apparatus, and tried to enter the cockpit, which was locked. He freed the canopy, holding it up with his neck, reached inside and brought out the youngest SAVED. He then reached for the elder SAVED, who was trapped by webbing. The youngest was brought to the surface and given m-mr (mouth-to-mouth resuscitation) by both FARRANT and CASSERLY, whilst in the water, and then transferred to a dinghy. The aircraft then completely sank, but not before FARRANT dived again to try to rescue the elder SAVED.

CASSERLY, besides resuscitating the youngest SAVED had tied a rope to a ring on the fuselage of the plane, whilst FARRANT was below the surface. Unfortunately the rope, which the crew of the *Rona* had been given, failed to hold and therefore the aircraft sank. HARBOR and FARRELL, in the dinghy, continued to give AR to the youngest SAVED, together with cardiac massage as the boy's heart appeared to have stopped. The boy was subsequently lifted by helicopter to hospital by the Royal Navy.

At 11.25 a second helicopter arrived and BAULD, a CPO diver jumped from 30 feet and descended 60 feet locating the wreckage of the plane and in a short time brought eldest SAVED to the surface. He was winched, apparently dead, by helicopter to hospital. However on board resuscitation was started and traces of life were found. In spite of desperate attempts to revive him he was finally pronounced dead at 14.00 hrs. The youngest boy subsequently died on 20th August.

Bronze Medal combined with Resuscitation Certificate voted to Farrant; Testimonial on Vellum combined with Resuscitation Certificate to Casserly; Testimonial on Vellum to Bauld; Resuscitation Certificates to Harbor and Farrell.

RE-OPENED CASE No. 77,635

This case was submitted as Case No. 6 by the Royal Humane Society for adjudication by the members of the Stanhope Gold Medal Committee on Monday 8th December 1980, whom recommended re-opening the Case to award a SILVER MEDAL in place of the BRONZE previously awarded on 4th March, 1980.

Bishop, Elizabeth, (23), Student Nurse　　　　　　　　　　　　　　　　　　　　　　　Case 78085

PLACE/ TIME:	Traffic Accident M2 Motorway, Bredgar, Sittingbourne, Kent.
	20th November 1980. 18.55 hrs.
CONDITIONS:	Due to road works London-bound traffic was channelled onto coastbound side of motorway. Contra-flow traffic therefore in operation.
SALVOR:	Elizabeth BISHOP (23) Student Nurse
SAVED:	Keith WILIAMS (36) Lorry Driver

SUMMARY:　　A double fatal accident occurred in which a heavy goods lorry driven by SAVED, London-bound, was crashed into by a saloon car. The lorry, fully loaded with coal shale, was partially embedded in an overhead bridge pillar, crushing the cab. Another saloon car was also involved. Both saloon car drivers lost their lives. SAVED trapped in his cab was screaming in pain and panic. BISHOP, a first year student at Kent and Canterbury Hospital, was an early arrival on the scene. On learning SAVED was trapped, without consideration for her own safety, BISHOP climbed into the crushed cab, the interior of which was covered in oils, blood and colliery shale, and comforted SAVED. During a two hour ordeal she was showered from time to time with shale and debris but remained with SAVED giving support, encouragement and sympathy. She rendered what aid was possible in horrific circumstances. Efforts were made to extricate SAVED from the wreckage necessitating pulling sections of the lorry apart - an operation presenting a certain danger both to SAVED and BISHOP. She however insisted on remaining at her post with SAVED. BISHOP, after SAVED was finally extricated, although mentally and physically exhausted, attempted to stay with SAVED, but was eventually persuaded to withdraw. Subsequently SAVED lost both his legs.

McQueen, Nicholas A.W., (28), Inspector, Hong Kong Police　　　　　　　　　　　　Case 78190

PLACE/ TIME:	The Southern Waters of Hong Kong, off Po Toi Island.
	23rd November 1979. 12.00 hrs.
CONDITIONS:	Strong NE Monsoon winds, 17 knots, broken wave height 4 to 10 feet with reverse ground swell from cliffs. Rescues about 50 yards from shore in 60 feet of water. Salvor swam about 50 yards.
SALVOR:	Police Inspector Nicholas Alexandre William McQUEEN (28)
	Royal Hong Kong Police Force
ASSISTANT:	Police Constable CHAN Shu-fai (19)
	Royal Hong Kong Police Force
SAVED:	47 Illegal Chinese Immigrants

SUMMARY:　　Two Marine Police launches went to the aid of a 40 foot sailing Junk which was drifting onto the rocks off Po Toi Island. A 45 foot launch managed to transfer 25 persons from the junk. The 78 foot launch commanded by McQueen started to tow the junk but soon a wave caught the junk abeam and it capsized. The occupants were thrown into the sea, and some 20 were saved. McQUEEN dived into the sea to help those clinging to the hull. It was then realised that there were people trapped inside. Wishing to turn the junk over, he felt underneath it for a fixture to which to secure a line, and fixed one round the sails and boom, but after the junk had rotated 30° the boom parted from the mast.

CHAN now joined him. The smaller launch returned and used it's vertical stem post to push and rotate the junk through 70°. One man scrambled out, but his clothing caught on something and he was pulled under as the junk rolled back. McQUEEN pulled him clear and he and CHAN got him to the launch. The junk was rolled again and another man came out, to be rescued by the two salvors.

Bronze Medal voted to Chan.

Buckfield, Donald R.J., (41), HM Coastguard　　　　　　　　　　　　　　　　　　　Case 78591

PLACE/ TIME:	Chough Zawn, Tatar Dhu, Lamorna.
	19th December 1981. 22.15 hrs.
CONDITIONS:	Sea very turbulent with waves of 40 feet. SE wind speed of 70-80 knots gusting to 100 knots. Ship *Union Star* drifted onto rocks near Tatar Dhu. Attempts to rescue crew by helicopter and Penlee lifeboat proved unsuccessful.
	See Summary.
ATTEMPTED SALVOR:	Donald Robert John BUCKFIELD (41) HM Coastguard

SUMMARY:　　When attempts to reach the *Union Star* by helicopter and Penlee lifeboat proved unsuccessful the Coastguard had called out the Penzance Sector Officer (BUCKFIELD) in charge of the Cliff Rescue Company. BUCKFIELD was directed to the cliffs where it was thought the *Union Star* was coming ashore. BUCKFIELDS journey to the site showed his determination, as his vehicle had broken down twice in the atrocious conditions. By good fortune a Post Office van came by on the second occasion and all the ropes and rescue gear were transferred to it. When BUCKFIELD arrived at the cliff top he directed the cliff Rescue Team where to set up equipment. Observing the *Union Star* with an auxiliary, both thought that they saw a man come out of the wheelhouse and enter the sea.

BUCKFIELD immediately put on the rescue harness with rope and was lowered over the cliff which at this point was approximately 60 feet high. The cliff was completely exposed to the very high gusting winds, and the waves were breaking at its foot, sending clouds of heavy spray the full height of the cliff. It was also raining very heavily at the time.

The only light available to BUCKFIELD was a hand held torch and other hand lamps held by the Cliff Rescue Team members not actually manning the ropes.

BUCKFIELD was lowered about half way down the cliff but could go no further because of the wave height. He remained in this very perilous position for some minutes endeavouring to locate any person in the water. He was then hauled back to the cliff top.

It was then decided to go to the base of a deep gully a short distance from the *Union Star*, as it was now known that the PENLEE LIFEBOAT was at least in danger if not lost, as there had been no radio contact for some time. A lifejacket of believed RNLI pattern was sighted.

BUCKFIELD decided to establish the origin of the lifebelt and was again lowered down the cliff, which, at this point, was 100 feet high. He was lowered to the base of the cliff, which was a little more sheltered. BUCKFIELD received considerable buffeting during this hazardous descent. BUCKFIELD was unable to recover the lifebelt but was able to confirm that it was RNLI pattern. BUCKFIELD after a further period of time was again hauled to the top of the cliff.

The report states that BUCKFIELD on both descents acted with complete disregard of his own safety; although he was attached to a rope he was in danger of being blown away from the cliff and severely injured.

BUCKFIELD then conferred with another Coastguard, he organised a search of the cliffs and remained on duty throughout the night.

At the inquest into the deaths of the crew of the Penlee Lifeboat and the *Union Star* the foreman of the jury commended BUCKFIELD for his actions and HM Coroner also associated himself with those remarks.

Pritchard, Margaret, (19), Taxi Driver   Case 78936

PLACE/ TIME:	A487 Porthmadog to Caernarfon Road, Penmorfa. 18th November 1982. 08.30 hrs.
CONDITIONS:	Weather damp and overcast with occasional showers. At the scene of the accident there was heavy fog. (Pritchard) estimated speed of vehicles in her direction as 30 mph.
Salvor	RESUSCITATION
SALVOR/ RESTORER:	Miss Margaret Eirian PRITCHARD (19) Taxi Driver Miss Sioned WILLIAMS (25) Teacher
A/SALVOR:	Simon Maurice Cooper JONES (24) Oil Depot Manager
SAVED:	Gwilyn HUMPHREYS (40) Petrol Tanker Driver Dewi Wyn JONES (-) Tipper Driver

SUMMARY: The accident is described from the point of view of PRITCHARD's vehicle as it occupied the central position. JONES (Dewi) was driving up a hill with the light on followed by PRITCHARD with dipped headlights. JONES (Dewi) pulled out to overtake a parked car followed by PRITCHARD. As PRITCHARD reached the parked car there was a loud crash & Jones (Dewi) lorry spun round, it's rear went over the opposite hedge and the front towards PRITCHARD's taxi. At this point HUMPHREYS's came down the hill out of the fog going across the road towards the near side, the articulated part of the tanker was at an angle. PRITCHARD saw a gap between rear of tanker and front of tipper, the gap was too narrow and the rear offside of her taxi caught the tipper.

PRITCHARD took her taxi out of the way and returned to the scene. PRITCHARD noticed that the tipper was on fire, she asked JONES (Dewi) if he had a fire extinguisher, which he had not. JONES (Dewi) was trapped by the legs and was screaming. PRITCHARD then went over to tanker to try to find a fire extinguisher. JONES (Simon) then arrived, found a small extinguisher and gave it to PRITCHARD, who went over to the tipper and put out the fire with it. There was a strong smell of petrol, so JONES (Simon) searched for and found a large fire extinguisher, which he took, and kept observation on the tanker in case fire should break out.

PRITCHARD had now returned to the tanker and was joined by WILLIAMS. The two SALVORS got hold of HUMPHREYS, who was unconscious and bleeding from head wounds. As he was gurgling they sat him up, opened his mouth and cleared it of blood. WILLIAMS took off her underslip to wipe the blood away from his head and from his mouth. Both SALVORS then made HUMPHREYS as comfortable as possible. HUMPHREYS was then removed and taken to hospital. JONES (Dewi) who was trapped could not be removed by cutting equipment due to the danger of fire and explosion, so the vehicle had to be broken manually. JONES (Dewi) was eventually removed to hospital.

Please Note that PRITCHARD in addition to her rescue efforts had turned off the Master Switch on the tanker (it had a full load of 6,000 gallons and lost 500 through leakage) and had taken the battery out of the tipper.

Testimonial on Vellum voted to Williams; Certificate of Commendation to Simon Jones.

Paley, Clifford W., (43), Sergeant, Sussex Police   Case 79141

PLACE/ TIME:	British Telecom House, Gloucester Place, Brighton. 4th December 1982. 20.45 hrs.
CONDITIONS:	Partly demolished Building. Wind SW - 18 knots. Force 4. Weather dry. Very dark. Rescue effected on seventh storey about 70 ft. from ground. See Summary.
SALVORS:	P.S. Clifford Watton PALEY (43) Insp. Michael John JUDGE (40) P.C. Stewart Ian COBLENZ (36) All Sussex Police.
SAVED:	Andrew Frank COCKERILL (19) Occupation not given.
SUMMARY:	Saved had an argument with his girlfriend, and climbed inside partly demolished building onto the seventh floor of the scaffolding (a scaffolding expert stated that the scaffolding being unfinished was particularly dangerous and that the building inside and out was not safe). The Fire Brigade who attended were unable to help as the turntable ladder was too heavy to be allowed to touch the building. The Police Officers climbed through the dark building using their torches and eventually reached the sixth floor, where they climbed onto the scaffolding lattice. There was a total absence of walking boards and safety rails. There SAVED was engaged in conversation by JUDGE & COBLENZ. PALEY moved to within 4 ft. of SAVED who was sitting near the end of an unsupported horizontal scaffold pole. PALEY maintained a conversation with SAVED for over 30 minutes, during which time the scaffolding was moving in an alarming way due to the wind and the weight of the men. SAVED was very irrational and if he had grappled with PALEY there would undoubtedly have been an appalling accident. Eventually SAVED was coaxed back into the building. The 3 SALVORS then had the difficult task of taking the highly emotional and irrational Youth down the inside of the partly demolished building to the ground. SAVED conveyed to Police Station.

Bronze Medals voted to Judge and Coblenz.

Golding, Victor Leonard, (39), Shift Supervisor   Case 79166

PLACE/ TIME:	Berks Spencer Acids Ltd., Canning Road, London E15. 22nd August, 1983. 02.15 hrs.
CONDITIONS:	See Summary.
SALVOR:	Victor Leonard Golding (39) Shift Supervisor
SAVED:	James Arthur APPS (30) Chemical Process Worker
SUMMARY:	SAVED & SALVOR were on the retort floor of the chemical works when one of the retorts exploded. Both were subjected to blast and severe acid burns, and were in danger from falling debris and from fire. SAVED was more severely injured but SALVOR although painfully injured and aware of the danger of further explosion and structural collapse, took the following action. SAVED was close to hysteria, so SALVOR, by use of persuasion and force guided SAVED out of the building. SALVOR then removed SAVED'S clothing, showered him down using an adjacent hose pipe, and then applied Bicarbonate of Soda Paste on his burns until the ambulance arrived.

SALVOR then proceeded to ensure that the plant was safe for the fire fighters, he isolated the gas valve at the rear of the plant. SALVOR then realised that a 500 gallon header of Sulphuric Acid might cause further danger, as fractured lines from it were spraying acid onto the retort floor. SALVOR therefore entered the plant again to isolate the dangerous and corrosive liquid. He virtually checked the drainage on all floors and in so doing subjected himself to injury from flying glass, spraying acid and falling debris. The shut-off valve was blocked so he had to drain down the header tank. He was successful in all these actions.

NOTE:- The plant suffered severe structural damage which necessitated the re-building of the retort.

Lawton, Frederick Arthur, (52), Auxiliary Plant Attendant Case 79261

PLACE/ TIME:	Skelton Grange Power Station, Pontefract Road, Leeds. 18th May, 1983. 12.00 hrs.
CONDITIONS:	See Summary.
SALVOR:	Frederick Arthur LAWTON (52) Auxiliary Plan t Attendant
SAVED:	Thomas Anthony DEAKIN (38) Foreman Boiler Cleaner
SUMMARY:	There are three main points to note:-

1. The actual rescue operation took 1_ hrs.
2. SAVED is a large man.
3. The Senior Fire Officer present stated that the conditions of the rescue were suicidal. In particular because SALVOR (LAWTON) was the only person able to enter the hopper because of his size.

The accident occurred as SAVED and another man were going to clean out the hopper. Because the hopper was very full, SAVED took off his safety harness. (This is contrary to instructions, which state that the man in the hopper has to wear his harness when he is in it and the safety man must remain, as his anchor man, outside the hopper). After SAVED had carried out certain safety tests, and as he was about to put on his harness, the crust suddenly gave way and he was thrown on his back in the hopper. The hydro-vac system drew him down, jamming both feet. SAVED blocked the system, dust unable to be exhausted from the bottom rapidly built up. Very quickly he was buried up to his head with only his outstretched arms being above dust level.

The alarm was raised and a number of people looked inside the hopper but could not see SAVED, even though lights had been lowered into it. LAWTON arrived, was told there was no hope of a rescue, but he looked in and saw SAVED's hands. LAWTON put on a safety harness and entered the hopper. (Police report states many people assisted from this point but none were ever in danger). LAWTON endeavoured to spread his weight, but still sank up to his knees. He dug down towards SAVED, by now buried; as he dug the dust flowed back, so he threw it into the air, holding one of SAVED's hands, as the visibility deteriorated. LAWTON eventually reached SAVED's mouth, as he did so SAVED collapsed. LAWTON again cleared the mouth and nose, at this point SAVED recovered and became hysterical. LAWTON managed to calm him.

SAVED now saw the wall of dust forming around LAWTON, so he told him to leave and let him die, as the wall might collapse at any moment. LAWTON refused, obtained a rope and tied it around SAVED's wrists. The rope was pulled by those outside, but failed to free saved, who was firmly wedged by his feet.

An air mask was passed down. LAWTON with great difficulty managed to secure it on SAVED and this action calmed SAVED.

An industrial vacuum with a 4 inch hose was passed down. LAWTON cut a ledge around the two of them and then cleared the dust from SAVED's shoulders. LAWTON continued doing this until he had cleared SAVED's shoulders completely. A safety harness was now lowered, LAWTON fixed it to SAVED and after further work SAVED was pulled free. LAWTON was then pulled up and as he went the accumulated dust suddenly collapsed taking all the lighting equipment with it. Both were removed to hospital, SAVED was discharged after treatment. LAWTON suffered severe cramp in his thighs for about a week.

Belshaw, Sarah Jane Esther, (22), Nurse Case 79652

PLACE/ TIME:	Site of pre-Inca temples of the Sun and Moon, Moche, Trujillo, Peru. 12th December 1984. Daytime
CONDITIONS:	See Summary.
SALVOR:	Miss Sarah Jane Esther BELSHAW (22) Nurse
SAVED:	Miss Christine MULLINS (24) Nurse
SUMMARY:	Trujillo, a city in the Peruvian coastal desert, is 650 kms north of Lima. SALVOR and SAVED, two British nurses, were visiting the site of pre-Inca temples at Moche, just outside Trujillo.

A small boy was at the site selling ceramics, which both SALVOR and SAVED were admiring. Suddenly, thieves or bandits attacked the boy, who managed to wriggle free and escape. The thieves then grabbed the nurses, demanded money, which they refused, and fired a shot. SAVED was hit, and SALVOR eventually saw that a bullet had entered her neck on the right and lodged in the left side. She was bleeding, began to have respiratory problems and turned blue. SALVOR started M to MR (mouth-to-mouth resuscitation) at the same time desperately looking round for help in this isolated area. SALVOR did not of course know if the thieves were still in the area - for over an hour she stayed protecting her friend, giving M to MR, and dashing out attempting to attract attention and help. Eventually, SALVOR attracted the attention of a villager with a horse and cart - SAVED was loaded onto the cart. SALVOR continued M to MR on the long trip across the desert towards Trujillo. SAVED was eventually transferred to a minibus and thence to hospital in Trujillo.

SAVED was evacuated from Trujillo to Lima, and thence by air to Miami, Florida. In Miami she went into a deep coma. SAVED is now back in hospital in England.

Her Britannic Majesty's Ambassador to Peru states: "Had she (SALVOR) not acted so selflessly, I have no doubt that her companion (SAVED) would have died on the spot before she ever got to hospital in Trujillo. I believe that the bravery and devotion displayed by (SALVOR) were of quite exceptional order and deserve a wider recognition".

Stevenson, Peter John, (59), Driver/ Care Assistant   Case 80609

PLACE/ TIME:	Watford Road, Sudbury, Wembley, Middlesex. 18th September, 1986. 16.15 hrs.
CONDITIONS:	See Summary.
SALVOR:	Peter John STEVENSON (59) Driver/ Care Assistant
A/SALVORS:	Mrs Pennie WOODHEAD (29) Housewife Miss Angela WILLIAMS (29) Housewife David Stephen SPARKS (28) AA Patrolman Paul John BARNHAM (26) Production Manager Miss Vanessa BALLARD (25) Grad. Marketing Executive Mrs. Jane WATTS (32) Telephonist Mrs. Brenda Joy KICK (-) Pt/time Sales Assistant
SAVED:	Mrs. Ellen CONNOR (87) Mrs. Ada SCOTT (82) Norman PARKER (72) Mrs, Gladys BENNETT (72) Mrs. Jessie WOOLLEY (70) later DECEASED
NOTES: at the	1. The ambulance was a specially converted Volkswagen ambulance with a side entrance and a tail lift rear entrance. 2. At the time of the accident, it carried a crew of 2 - STEVENSON, the SALVOR and WAUMSLEY, an escort who disappeared and has not been seen since. 3. There were 10 passengers - 8 strapped into seats and 2 in wheelchairs clamped to the floor. It is fair to assume that the correct total of SAVED should read 10 rather than 5 as named. 4. After a brief description of the incident, each SALVOR/ A/SALVOR has a small paragraph to indicate the part they appeared to play in the incident. Without denigrating the report in any way, it is very confused due to the great confusion at the scene, added to which most statements say "I was very confused and frightened and cannot recall clearly what happened."

SUMMARY: STEVENSON was driving the ambulance containing SAVED, all of whom were elderly and frail. He noticed a strong smell of petrol and then there was a loud bang. He pulled in to the side and noticed flames coming from the engine compartment. Having stopped the vehicle, STEVENSON ran to the rear to engage the power lift for the wheelchairs. He then went to the near side to evacuate SAVED from front as fire had already come into the vehicle. He saved SCOTT and CONNER, entering the vehicle for each one. Black smoke and intensive (sic) heat now made the situation very dangerous and STEVENSON received 1st and 2nd degree burns to his hands. He continued and pulled out WOOLLEY, who weighed 14 stone, was on fire and very slow-moving due to a stroke. STEVENSON went back and rescued PARKER. STEVENSON repeatedly entered the vehicle until he was sure that all his passengers were safe.

WOODHEAD, with KICK and their 4 children, was approaching the van in her car from the opposite direction. They noticed van was on fire, so stopped and ran back. WOODHEAD helped STEVENSON with rescue of PARKER. She could not get into van as the flames were so bad. She helped also with WOOLLEY and SPARKS joined her. She helped in rescue generally.

WILLIAMS was apparently on foot. She actually braved the fire and got into the van to help STEVENSON. She undoubtedly took a considerable part in the rescue. In her statement she mentions that SPARKS had entered the van and was assisting in getting SAVED out.

SPARKS helped STEVENSON with one wheelchair SAVED, probably PARKER. AS stated above, SPARKS braved fire and smoke to get in the van. A number of SALVORS mention him as being a SALVOR who worked hard. He was easy to recognise in his uniform.

BARNHAM was in his car with BALLARD and ran back to assist. He tried to move a wheelchair (he must therefore have entered van) without success, then found out how to release it and carried it out. BARNHAM no doubt took further part in the rescue but cannot recall clearly as he was confused.

BALLARD found one of SAVED on bottom step of van and pulled her away to safety. BALLARD continued to assist generally in pulling SAVED to safety.

KICK (not put up by police) was with WOODHEAD in her car. Her first act was to ensure that the Fire Brigade had been summoned. KICK assisted WILLIAMS in removing one SAVED to safety. She helped STEVENSON with one of the wheelchair SAVED, and then assisted generally.

WATTS (not put up by police) was in her car with her 2 children. Saw van before it stopped, noticed the fire and flashed her lights and blew her horn. She assisted in the rescue generally. She put her children in WOODHEAD's car and took 3 SAVED home (probably those un-named).

In conclusion: Every single witness stated that the work of STEVENSON was quite outstanding. His thoughts and actions were for his passengers. He repeatedly faced the horrors of fire and smoke, receiving severe burns to his hands. The original police report suggested that he should be considered for a Sovereign's award.

Testimonial on Vellum voted to Woodhead, Williams, Sparks and Barnham, Testimonial on Parchment to Ballard and Kick; Certificate of Commendation to Watts.

Berriff, Paul, (42), Television Producer   Case 81025

PLACE/ TIME:	"The Old Man of Stoer", Stoerhead, nr. Lochinver, Sutherland. 27th October 1988. 23.30 hrs.
CONDITIONS: fall of	Channel of about 50 feet between 250 feet high stack and the bottom of 300 feet high cliff. The rise and the sea in the channel was about 8 feet; boiling seas in the channel with the result that the entire area was covered in deep white sea foam. Salvor did not actually swim, as he was attached to a rope, but he was continuously immersed during the rescue.
SALVOR:	Paul BERRIFF (42) Television Producer
A/SALVORS:	Philip Stanley JONES (46) Stores Assistant
	Janey Heap O'NEIL (21) Potter
	Steve Heap O'NEIL (27) Pottery Worker
	Ian Ross MACLEOD (30) Joiner
	All 4 members of the Assynt Mountain Rescue Team
SAVED:	Nigel John DEUDNEY (22) Student
SUMMARY:	ALLAN, NEWCOMBE and DEUDNEY were members of Stirling University Mountaineering Club intending to climb the "Old Man of Stoer". On their descent, the weather worsened considerably and the party had difficulty with their ropes. ALLAN succeeded in crossing a rope from the "Old Man of Stoer" to the mainland, leaving NEWCOMBE and DEUDNEY on stack and went to raise the alarm.

Police, Coastguard and Assynt Mountain Rescue Team assembled at cliff top. RAF Rescue Helicopter arrived and reported one climber (NEWCOMBE) was attached to traverse rope, apparently dead. SAVED was at base of stack attached to a rope and continually buffeted and submerged by breaking waves.

BERRIFF was on board the SAR Helicopter making a documentary TV series about the work of the Rescue Flight. When helicopter dropped the Mountain Rescue Team at the top of the cliff, BERRIFF and his sound recordist jumped out. The Rescue Team abseiled down the face of cliff to carry out a recce and sent back a message requesting a boat hook to remove the dead body from the traverse rope.

BERRIFF now suggested to MRT that as he was wearing a dry suit and a life jacket he might be useful in assisting in the rescue (BERRIFF is an auxiliary coastguard in Hull so has some experience in cliff rescue).

BERRIFF now borrowed a climbing harness from MRT and abseiled down cliff. He then attached some Karrabiner clips to the rope and moved on to the traverse rope. A large knot in the rope took some time to overcome, during which time he was constantly buffeted by waves and submerged. On arrival at body, he clipped a safety line to it and signalled the rescue team to haul them both in. Body was taken off rope.

BERRIFF then set off again across the rope to the "Old Man of Stoer". Helicopter used searchlights to flood area with light. SALVOR was constantly submerged in worsening sea. When he reached the stack, he was knocked against the rocks. He clambered up to SAVED, who was in an extremely poor condition, being attached to the base by a belay and clinging desperately to rope. BERRIFF untied him and clipped him on to traverse rope and inflated his life jacket which was fitted with a light and locator beacon. SAVED and SALVOR were pulled across by MRT.

SAVED was now in danger of becoming unconscious due to hypothermia. MRT worked to keep him conscious. BERRIFF radioed to helicopter to lift them, but the helicopter cable was only 250 feet long. BERRIFF and MRT stretchered SAVED 50 feet up cliff to an outcrop of rock where helicopter was able to lower cable and lift SAVED who was then helicoptered to hospital.

Testimonial on Vellum voted to Jones, J. O'Neil, S. O'Neil and MacLeod.

Thorne, Bryan John, (49), Ambulanceman   Case 81302

PLACE/ TIME:	Locks Drove, Upton, Andover, Kent.
	19th September, 1989. 12.31 hrs.
CONDITIONS:	Injury occurred over 100 feet up a 150 feet radio tower. SAVED dropped onto a triangular steel mesh at 100 feet.
SALVOR:	Ambulanceman Bryan John THORNE (49) Hampshire Ambulance Service
A/SALVORS:	Gary WEST (22) Rigger
SAVED:	Tony BLUNDEN (44) Rigger
SUMMARY:	SAVED, working some 110 feet up radio mast, was hit on head by a chunk of metal, which gave him a compound fracture and took out his left eye.

THORNE was first man to answer call for assistance. He suffers very severely from vertigo and had to stop 3 times on his way up mast to reinforce his courage to continue. He took a number of dressings, a jacket (wind was cold and gusty) and a safety body strap.

On arrival at top, THORNE found SAVED being attended by WEST. THORNE attached his safety strap, gave SAVED first aid for his serious wounds and lashed him to the net. SAVED was in addition vomiting blood and stomach contents. THORNE appreciated the only method of rescue was by a paraguard stretcher, which was brought up.

Others were now assisting with the rescue. SAVED was winched down and removed to hospital. THORNE was now suffering so much from vertigo that he had to be attached to a safety line and lowered to safety.

Testimonial on Parchment voted to West.

Saunders, Norman Douglas, (47), Draughtsman/ Designer   Case 81319

PLACE/ TIME:	A286 Chichester/ Midhurst Road, Singleton, Sussex.
	30th July 1989. 23.15 hrs.
CONDITIONS:	Road Traffic Accident - See Summary.
SALVOR:	Norman Douglas SAUNDERS (47) Draughtsman/ Designer
SAVED:	Miss Katie Jane FLOOK (23) Receptionist
ATTEMPTED SAVED:	Gary SWEET (27) Occupation not given DECEASED
SUMMARY:	SAUNDERS was a front seat passenger in a car being driven by his wife. At the end of the village of Singleton there is a right hand bend and a road junction. A/SAVED came from the opposite direction driving very fast (reputedly over 50 mph in a 30 mph area and on the wrong side of the road). Mrs. Saunders turned her vehicle to her offside to avoid a head-on collision. A/SAVED's car passed on her nearside, continued on the grass verge, hitting a large tree head on. Mrs Saunders stopped her car putting on her hazard lights.

SAUNDERS ran back and tried to open the passenger door, as flames were already reaching inside of car. It was jammed but the window was slightly open and he was able to wrench door open. SAVED had undone her safety belt so SAUNDERS pulled her out and dragged her away from car as flames intensified.

SAUNDERS returned to car and tried to rescue A/SAVED from passenger side as offside door was jammed but was beaten back by flames. Within seconds there was a huge explosion and the car was engulfed in flames.

SAVED was removed to hospital and detained.

Benfield, Mark David, (26), Shopfitter   Case 82108
Giles, Michael Kenneth, (33), Electrician
Mildon, Leslie John, (60), Company Director

PLACE/ TIME:	M4 East Garston-Membury, Hungerford, Berks.
	13th March 1991. 06.50 hrs.

CONDITIONS:	Foggy - opinions vary about visibility from 100 to 200 yards. Speeds approaching scene varied considerably from inside to outside lane. Speeds in inside lane were between 40 and 45 mph, outside lane between 70 and 90 mph.	
NOTES:	Attached to report is police sketch plan with vehicle numbers allotted to them (not reproduced here). Vehicle occupants are shown below. Police report gives long statements from most people involved in saving and attempting to save life. Vehicles involved were 50, 30 being damaged or destroyed. Below is given a short description of most Salvors' actions with MILDON, BENFIELD and GILES being particularly recommended for outstanding bravery.	
	It is worth noting that the Asst. Chief Fire Officer is reported as saying that it is not normal for professional fire-fighters to receive awards unless their conduct is outside their normal conduct or training. Furthermore it is procedure that the crew is considered as a whole rather than as individuals.	
SAVED:	John NESSLING (46) Lorry driver	V 41
	Mrs Pauline Anne STOCK (47) Self employed	V 29
	Arthur James HANCOCK (62) retired	V 29
	Cpl. Miles WEBB (28) Royal Signals	V 7
A/SAVED	Graham BRANCH (-) Occ. Not known	V 3
	5 men in Renault Van (1 WRIGHT)	V 46?
	- DEACON (-) no details	V 45
	- ANCONA (-) no details	V 46
	- GOULD-DAVIS (-) no details	V 12
	1 OTHER (not named)	V ?
SALVORS:	of NESSLING	EVERISS, HENCHER, SANDO, Sig. SCOTT, VINCENT, HANCOCK, HASTINGS, MacDONALD, PC BECK, PC LEECH, 5 named
FIREMEN		
	of STONE & HANCOCK	BENFIELD, HENCHER, PHILLIPS
	of Cpl. WEBB	L/Cpl TINDAL, Sig. SCOTT, BENFIELD, MacDONALD
ATTEMPTING		
SALVORS:	of BRANCH	PC COOPER, PHILLIPS, MILDON
	of UNKNOWN MEN	GILES, PIERCE, MILDON
SUMMARY:	All SALVORS' names have been put in alphabetical order, as some are engaged in more than one rescue. Police and Fire personnel appear together. Where vehicle numbers of Salvors are available, they are quoted.	

Mark David BENFIELD (26) Shopfitter V 23
Mark Richard HENCHER (23) Shopfitter V 23

Both travelling in Ford Minibus (with driver and 2 others not recommended). All travelling to Gatwick. BENFIELD and HENCHER saw fire start in nearby vehicle. They saw Mrs STONE's vehicle and that she had severe facial injuries. They tried to open her door without success, but they managed to open rear offside door and pulled her clear. PHILLIPS also assisted in this rescue. HANCOCK was also released by them. HENCHER also assisted in releasing NESSLING. BENFIELD assisted in releasing Cpl. Webb. BENFIELD suffered heat from fires here.

Testimonial on Vellum voted to Hencher.

Frederick Ian EVERISS (42) HGV Driver V 42

Drove onto hard shoulder to avoid accident, which was a fruitless effort as he was struck in the rear by another lorry. Although extremely shaken and dazed, he checked his lorry. He saw driver of lorry (V 41) NESSLING was trapped. There was an explosion nearby and flames appeared. EVERISS continued to try to release NESSLING, being shielded from flames by a coat. A fireman arrived with cutting tools and EVERISS and others freed NESSLING. He stayed with NESSLING until ambulance arrived.

Testimonial on Vellum voted to Everiss.

FIRE (WHITE WATCH - 5 names mentioned out of 8 crew)
Sub Officer John CAMERON (40)
Leading Firefighter Christopher Leonard COLING (21)
Firefighter Christopher John BRIDGEMAN (-)
Firefighter Brian Raymond TUBB (-)
Firefighter George Peter SETTER (-)
All of Royal Berkshire Fire and Rescue Service

CAMERON was the officer i/c of first fire appliance to reach the scene. He appreciated the situation, realised scale of incident and deployed his crew. He saw that NESSLING was the person his crew were well qualified to rescue. He ordered to F/Fs to take cutting gear to Vehicle 41. Cameron and a police officer used a portable generator to operate rescue gear. F/Fs used hoses to damp down fires. The conditions were very hot and almost untenable. Cameron and his crew carried out all the work they could and CAMERON than withdrew his crew to safety.

Team Vellum voted to White Watch.

Michael Kenneth GILES (33) Electrician V 8

GILES was the driver of a Ford Van. When the vehicle came to a rest he got out by the nearside and went up the embankment. He was joined by his passenger who had a cut head. GILES saw a man trapped in a van, went down and assisted unnamed man to release driver. Both tried to pull man out of van. They succeeded in freeing the top half of his body but his legs remained trapped. BENFIELD now arrived and assisted GILES, both SALVORS suffering considerably from the fire. Fortunately a Salvor with a fire extinguisher put out the flames on their clothes.

Mark Richard HENCHER (23) - see BENFIELD above

Arthur James HANCOCK (62) retired V 29

HANCOCK, a passenger in car driven by STONE, was rescued by BENFIELD and HENCHER, see above. HANCOCK then went with others to assist in releasing NESSLING. He was then taken to hospital by ambulance.

Testimonial on Vellum voted to Hancock.

Dean Bryan HASTINGS (31) Block Paver V 18
Howard David VINCENT (35) Self employed V 18

HASTINGS was driver and VINCENT passenger in a van. Both assisted in the release of NESSLING and were affected quite considerably by the heat and flames from nearby fires.

Testimonials on Vellum voted to Hastings and Vincent.

Leslie John MILDON (60) Company Director V 20

MILDON was driving alone and was able to stop his vehicle without colliding with anyone else. Unfortunately he was hit from behind and shunted onto vehicle in front. He climbed out of his car through nearside window. He joined GILES and PEARCE in trying to release a man (probably WRIGHT - Deceased). They released the upper body of man and MILDON stood on another vehicle to assist his efforts. His clothes caught fire and PEARCE extinguished the flames. MILDON continued and again his clothes caught fire, extinguished by SCOTT. MILDON's hair and eyebrows then caught fire and he was forcibly removed by TINDAL. MILDON then assisted in the removal of BRANCH.

Peter John MacDONALD (43) Project Manager V 17

One of the many who assisted in the rescue of NESSLING. Once that had been completed, he helped in the rescue of Cpl WEBB (V 7) again with others. Police did not obtain a statement from him so there are no further details.

Testimonial on Vellum voted to MacDonald.

Nigel PEARCE (27) HGV Driver V 6

He was involved in accident and assisted MILDON and GILES in attempting to release a trapped driver, protecting them by using a fire extinguisher. He also helped to extinguish flames on BENFIELD's clothes.

Testimonial on Vellum voted to Pearce.

Robert John PHILLIPS (42) Regional Sales Manager

His vehicle was not involved in the accident. He walked along the line of vehicles and assisted in the rescue of HANCOCK. He also assisted others in the release of a lorry driver (probably NESSLING). PHILLIPS assisted generally in moving vehicles and preventing explosions taking place.

Testimonial on Vellum voted to Phillips.

POLICE (All Thames Valley Police)
Police Constable Roger Ian COOPER

A single crew landrover driver, he was the first police officer on the scene, He found BRANCH trapped in his vehicle. He hitched his vehicle to BRANCH's and towed it clear. Eventually with others he assisted to pull BRANCH out, but sadly he was dead. COOPER then continued to carry out the organisation and control of the rescue work.

Police Constable Gary BECK (29)
Police Constable Christopher Martin LEECH (34)

LEECH and another officer (Grey, not recommended) were the crew of a police vehicle. GREY assessed situation, realised numbers of people were trapped and shouted to LEECH to bring a crowbar. They saw BECK trying to release a trapped driver (probably NESSLING). LEECH assisted by wedging a crowbar under the seat. Heat from fire was intense. Firemen with cutting gear arrived and the driver was released.

Testimonials on Vellum to Cooper, Beck and Leech.

Arthur Francis SANDO (59) British Rail Supervisor V 39

Driver of a Ford van in centre of incident. He climbed out through his shattered windscreen. Saw NESSLING trapped, shouted for assistance and went to vehicle. Heat from a nearby fire was intense. With others he rescued NESSLING.

Testimonial on Vellum voted to Sando.

Signalman Craig Robert SCOTT (18) Royal Signals V 7
L/Cpl Stephen Mark TINDAL (23) Royal Signals V 7

Both passengers in an army landrover driven by Cpl WEBB, who was knocked unconscious in the accident. TINDAL released himself and WEBB from seat belts but WEBB was trapped. TINDAL took a sledgehammer to release WEBB and then noticed a man trapped in a van. TINDAL and SCOTT went to release this man. Fire was very close and SCOTT used his fire extinguisher. WEBB had now released himself but could not get out of vehicle and TINDAL and SCOTT pulled him out. As stated above, BENFIELD had been active in this rescue. Both TINDAL and SCOTT continued to give assistance to others at scene.

Testimonials on Vellum to Scott and Tindal.

Sloane, Christopher   Case 83676

Details witheld for legal reasons.

Cochrane, Raymond, Jockey   Case 84081

PLACE/ TIME:	Newmarket Racecourse, Suffolk.
	1st June 2000.
CONDITIONS:	Plane crash.
SALVOR:	Raymond COCHRANE Jockey
SAVED:	Frankie DETTORI Jockey
ATTEMPTED SAVED:	Patrick MACKAY Pilot DECEASED 1st June 2000
SUMMARY:	COCHRANE and SAVED were passengers in a Piper Seneca aircraft piloted by A/SAVED. After taking off, the pilot experienced difficulties and the plane crashed, catching fire.

COCHRANE escaped through the luggage hatch. SAVED was concussed and had a broken ankle; he was fastened by his harness and trapped in the burning plane. COCHRANE got him out and dragged him to safety. He then returned to the plane and managed to open the cockpit door but was unable to rescue A/SAVED.

COCHRANE was treated in hospital for burns to his hands and face and for internal injuries. (He has since had to give up riding as a result of his injuries).

Robertson, Keith, (37), Self-employed Lorry Driver   Case 84099

PLACE/ TIME:	Near Woodheads Farm, Lauder.
	15th October 2000. 14.10 hrs.
CONDITIONS:	Fatal multiple RTA.
SALVOR:	Keith ROBERTSON (37) Self-employed lorry driver.

SAVED: Richard HONER (38)
                      Mandy HONER (33)
                      Richard HONER (5)
                      Courtney HONER (3)

SUMMARY: Two cars, each with two elderly occupants, collided on a dual carriageway. One car overturned. The other

                      crossed the central reservation onto the wrong carriageway and collided head-on with a third car, and came to rest on its roof killing both occupants.

The HONER family were severely injured and trapped in the third car, which started to ignite.

ROBERTSON in his lorry was approaching and saw the accident. He stopped, ran to the car and managed to open the front nearside door. However, from there he saw that the driver was trapped by his legs with flames getting closer so he went round and tried to open that door, but could only do so partially.

ROBERTSON, as quickly as he could, got Mrs HONER (who had a broken femur) out and dragged her clear, then got the two children out of the back. He made another attempt to get Mr HONER out but could still not open the door any further. He ran to his lorry to phone for help and returned to the car. Mr HONER had managed to squeeze his upper body through the door gap; his trousers and T-shirt were on fire. After a prolonged struggle, ROBERTSON managed to get him out and drag him to safety.

By the time the Fire Brigade and ambulance arrived, the car was well alight. All members of the family were taken to hospital with serious injuries, Mr HONER sustaining 40% burns to his legs and abdomen.

R.H.S. BRONZE MEDALS WITH CLASPS

The Royal Humane Society
Clasps

From its earliest days, the Society had been faced with the problem of rewarding individuals who, in performing further acts of gallantry, earned the Society's medal on more than one occasion. This presented no problems whilst the large medals were still being awarded, as a second medal could be given to the rescuer. After 1869 however, the Society had to contend with the fact that their medals were now being worn on uniform and accordingly proposed to the army that, in future, individuals entitled to a second Royal Humane Society medal should receive instead a clasp to be worn on the ribbon of their existing award[5].

The army's response was positive, W.F. Forster replying on behalf of the Commander in Chief on 22 March 1869 that '...His Royal Highness sees no objection to the proposal, and will cause the same to be made known to the Army by a General Order...' The letter added that the Secretary of State for War was likewise agreeable to the proposal, and that a similar General Order would be issued to the Navy.

The Society's medallists, R. Warrington & Co., were accordingly approached for designs for the clasp and design 'A' was duly adopted. This took the form of a central oval bearing the initials R.H.S., from which drooped two scrolls upon which could be engraved details of the rescue for which it was awarded.

Warrington's continued to supply the Society with clasps until 1897, in which year the contract passed to Elkington & Co.[6] Several minor varieties exist, differing primarily in the method by which they were attached to the ribbon of the medal.

Clasps were struck both in silver and in bronze. It is worthy of note that silver clasps were issued to holders of silver medals, irrespective of whether the deed for which the clasp was awarded was of silver or of bronze standard. The reason for this appears to have been purely aesthetic, it being felt that[7]:

> *In order to avoid the incongruity of Silver Medals being worn with Bronze Clasps ... Silver Clasps be granted to Silver Medallists in cases where Bronze only would otherwise be awarded, but such grants shall not affect awards of Vellum or Parchment Testimonials respectively in Cases to which they were applicable.*

---

[5] Marjory Robson, 'Clasps to the Royal Humane Society Medals', *Life Saving Awards Research Society Journal* 24 (1995), pp. 4-20, hereafter cited as Robson, 'Clasps'.

[6] Robson, 'Clasps', p. 12.

[7] RHS Committee Minutes, 16 Nov. 1869.

A total of 17 silver and 248 bronze clasps have been awarded. No silver clasps have been awarded since 1917, whilst the last bronze clasp was won in 1950[8].

	MEDAL		**CLASP**		
Name	Case No.	Year	Case No.	Year	Notes
Adams, William	25160	1890	29729,30,31	1898	
			30217	1899	2nd Clasp
			30791	1900	3rd Clasp
Alder, William N.	43058	1916	45037	1919	
Allistone, John	25104	1890	31074	1900	
Andrews, W.D.	21420	1881	21823	1882	*[1]
			22181	1883	2nd Clasp
Bamber, Walter Leigh	17279	1864	18600	1870	
Barrett, Richard	27323	1894	36559	1909	
Barry, Michael	43139	1917	43653	1917	
Beadle, Robert Graham	26858	1893	33043	1903	
Bear, Thomas Walter	24701	1889	30576	1900	
Bell, Richard R.G.	29036	1897	40115	1913	
Beresford, Lord Chas. W. D	17182	1863	18722	1871	
Berry, Ernest Reginald	53538	1936	53623	1936	
Beveridge, Alexander	18046	1867	18482	1870	
Blackmore, M.H.	34548	1906	34692	1906	
Blake, Stephen	18706	1871	22788	1885	
Bolt, John	21844	1882	22456	1884	
Bone, John J.	18265	1868	18941	1872	
Booth, Arthur C.	37094	1909	42945	1916	
Bowen, Henry	25821	1892	29682	1898	
Bradley, William	21705	1882	22089	1883	*[2]
			23977	1888	2nd Clasp
Brinkworth, George	23455	1887	39936	1913	
Bromley, Arthur	32512	1903	35712	1907	
Brookes, G.C.	19662	1875	20748	1879	
Brown, William T.	42263	1916	46216	1921	
Brunnen, James	17985	1867	24861	1890	
Bryce (Brice), John Vincent	24283	1889	24768	1890	
Buchan, Arthur G.	38083	1911	39493	1912	
Bull, John	18291	1869	18304	1869	
Burke, Henry F.	26352	1893	27833	1895	
Butters, Rev Wm. Middleton	21783	1882	22817	1885	
Byrne, Henry	29229	1897	29254	1897	
Campbell, Duncan	31204	1901	31450	1901	
Carpendale, Trevor M.	43338	1917	55204	1939	

---

[8] A complete roll of these recipients has been published. See Robson 'Clasps'. A second silver clasp has been earned on only one occasion, whilst 13 second, 4 third, 4 fourth and a single fifth bronze clasps have been awarded.

Name					
Carr, John James	30684	1900	30801	1900	
			32150	1902	2nd Clasp
			33297	1904	3rd Clasp
			39009	1912	4th Clasp
Carruthers, John T.	27983	1895	34588	1906	
Cavill, Frederick	18259	1868	18641	1870	
Ceil(e)y, George R.	21810	1882	25635	1891	
Channer, George K.	27280	1894	31300	1901	
Channon, Samuel	18167	1868	19427	1874	
Churchill, William.	18398	1869	18792	1871	
Clowes, Alfred	33164	1904	34785	1906	
Coleman, Albert E.	21169	1880	21966	1883	
			22989	1886	2nd Clasp
Congdon, George T.	22935	1885	28723	1897	
Cook, David E.	22211	1883	23257	1886	
			23369	1886	2nd Clasp
			26253	1893	3rd Clasp
Cosh, Henry	28723	1897	34758	1906	
Craig, George	26947	1894	27401	1894	
			31067	1900	2nd Clasp
Craner, Edward	19204	1873	20197	1877	
Crichton, James	18800	1871	18800	1871	
Cruttenden, Frank Percy	61366	1950	61498	1950	
Curtis, Thomas E.	22523	1884	23445	1887	
Dacres, Seymour Henry P.	17510	1865	19632	1875	
Davis, Frederick J.	21620	1882	22382	1884	
Davis, Snowden	22919	1885	23438	1887	
Donohue, Daniel	18870	1872	19652	1875	
Douglas, Henry	17910	1867	21609	1882	
Drake, Rev.H.M.	29194	1897	29418	1898	
Drane, Robert	29807	1898	30144	1899	
			31490	1901	2nd Clasp
			31805	1902	3rd Clasp
			36919	1909	4th Clasp
Dryden, James	27636	1893	29618	1898	
Dulon, Martin	23430	1887	24038	1888	
Dunbar, Herman	42849	1916	46631	1922	
Edwards, Albert	37960	1911	38848	1912	
Ellard, Joseph	24657	1889	31620	1901	
Enderstein, Seigfred M.	40681	1914	40681	1914	
Falconer, Joseph	23839	1888	28117	1895	
Fant, John	51292	1932	52568	1934	
Ferguson, W.	21479	1881	21540	1881	
Fieldhouse, Walter	18618	1870	18686	1871	
Finnis, James W.	34004	1905	37922	1910	

Name					
Fippin(g), Ernest	22551	1884	25068	1890	
Fisher, William Blake	21925	1883	22655	1885	
Fitch, Walter	33186	1904	33735	1905	
Flemyng, Archibald E.F.	22132	1883	27745	1895	
Foot(e), Thomas	16308(a)	1858	24048	1888	
Foster, George	21428	1881	23105	1886	
Freeland, Alfred	18998	1872	19551	1875	
Fullick, Edward	28036	1895	32456	1903	
Gladding, George	32022	1902	33872	1905	
Glasson, Thomas S.	28975	1897	31099	1901	
Goldsmith, Henry	22271	1884	32336	1902	
Gonsalves, Manoel	46686	1923	47648	1925	
Gornall, Henry	16549	1860	23426	1887	
Grace, Edward	28695	1897	32898	1903	
Grant, Richard S.	35405	1907	38316	1911	
Gray, H.C.B.	20829	1880	28222	1896	
Gregory, Thomas R.	26593	1893	30010	1899	
Griffiths, Thomas	16294	1859	19683	1875	
Grunsell, W.H.	21521	1881	30066	1899	
Hammet, James L.	19581	1875	22679	1885	
Hellyer, Edwin A.	28256	1896	29059	1897	
Henderson, Arnott	19527	1874	19778	1875	
Herd, Robert	26014	1892	26607	1893	
Hodgson, Joseph R.	19052	1872	20959	1880	
Hollingsworth, E.	38249	1911	39752	1913	
Holloway, Graham C.	33039	1903	34287	1905	
Holt, Hugh W.L.	17850	1866	19135	1873	*3
Hood, James Samuel	19834	1876	22243	1884	
Hooton, James W.	18348	1869	18682	1871	
Hugill, Henry J.	18813	1874	19319	1874	
Humphries, Charles	22868,69	1885	23931	1888	
Hunt, Hubert H.	39174	1912	40587	1914	
Huntingford, W.	30189	1899	33320	1904	
Hurcum, Charles	34427	1906	34539	1906	
Isaacs, Henry J.	23091	1886	25635	1891	
Jappy, James	41455	1915	41455	1915	2nd Clasp *4
			41455	1915	3rd Clasp *4
Jermyn, John	21344	1881	22309	1884	
			24386	1889	2nd Clasp
Johns, John	23765	1887	29042	1897	
Jubb, Benjamin B.	40583	1914	42940	1916	
Jutelet, J.G.	16350	1859	19143	1873	
Kemsley, H.H.	41883	1915	41884	1915	
Lamport, Frederick W.	19867	1876	42616	1916	
Langdale, Frederick Lenox	19399	1874	20089	1877	
Langdon, Fredk Gilbert Chas	19399	1874	30976	1900	

Name	Number	Year	Number	Year	Clasp
Langton, George	21334,35	1881	22214	1884	
Lawrey, George	26905	1894	26906	1894	
Leonard, Peter	23716	1887	24142	1888	
Lipscombe, Alfred	20440	1878	21791	1882	
Little, George	25714	1891	26208	1892	
			26900	1893	2nd Clasp
			29460	1898	3rd Clasp
Litton, James J.	20079	1877	20347,48	1878	
Long, Frederick	21477	1881	24078	1888	
Lovering, Richard	18090	1868	22617	1885	
Luccock, Thomas	15060	1851	19236	1873	
Mallon, Michael	26524	1893	33745	1905	
Martin, Robert W.	30839	1900	40632	1914	
Martins, Robert	19826	1876	20003	1876	
			23341	1886	2nd Clasp
M(a)cAdam, Francis R.P.	21355	1881	25840	1892	
McAlister, William	21803	1882	25049	1890	
McGhee, W.	20933	1880	21497	1881	
McLeod, Donald	40548	1913	42282	1916	
McLeod, Malcolm	54007	1937	55306	1939	
McVay, M.	27836	1895	28032	1895	
Moat, William	19279	1873	22057	1883	
Monger, Harold G.R.	46767	1923	47868	1925	
Montgomery, Donald	18746	1871	20041	1876	
Moss, Josiah W.	23484	1887	25533	1891	
Neilson, Isaac	35279	1907	36499	1909	
Neno, John	17345	1864	18551	1870	
Neville, Richard John	22071	1883	22731	1885	
Newsham, John	39335	1912	40229	1913	
Newton, Hilary E.	26863	1893	34773	1906	
Noble, Andrew	22954	1885	22955	1885	
Noel, Montague Wriothesley	42270	1916	43853	1917	
North, Richard	23543	1887	26309	1893	
			27751	1895	2nd Clasp
O'Connor, Patrick	21276	1881	22607	1884	
O'Sullivan, Charles	21160	1880	22230	1884	
Oakes, W.E.	18935	1872	19115/19192	1873	
Oliver, William M.	18742	1871	18742	1871	
Panchen, Charles	20221	1877	22078	1883	
Paton, Thomas	18887	1872	19459	1874	
Peebles, George	22096	1883	22097	1883	
Pengelly, Ernest	42743	1916	43917	1918	
Petty, George	18507	1870	18565	1870	
Phelps, Frederick	17503	1865	23916	1888	
Philpin, Richard	24709	1889	29368	1898	
Pigg, Joseph	21914	1883	22360	1884	

Name					
Pocklington, A.J.	19715	1875	20275	1877	
Poë, Edmund Samuel	19632	1875	20047	1876	
Potter, James	18621	1870	19408	1874	
Prescott, John	22335	1884	26865	1893	
Prinsep, J.F.M.	22686	1885	23020	1886	
Pritchard, Robert	18320	1869	19407	1874	
Puttock, Robert	23391	1887	23906	1888	
Quigley, Patrick	18276	1869	18855	1872	
Quince, J.	20215	1877	21703	1882	*[5]
Renforth, Stephen	25070	1890	27537	1895	
			30122	1899	2nd Clasp
Rix, James	18728	1871	22022	1883	
Robe, John	19164	1873	22770	1885	
Roberts, Ben	20398	1878	20822	1880	
Robertson, R.	36202	1908	36904	1909	
Ross, A.D.	14703	1849	19182	1873	
Rowland, Alexander	26197	1892	27052	1894	
Sailing, Laurence (Lawrence)	33277	1904	39964	1913	
Sandilands, Hon Francis R.	19593	1875	22602	1884	
Sayce, Henry	35280	1907	44619	1918	
Sayer, Henry	25850	1892	25894	1892	
			26463	1893	2nd Clasp
			26603	1893	3rd Clasp
			27727,28	1895	4th Clasp
			37048	1909	5th Clasp
Scaife, Henry Neale	14988	1850	19097	1873	
Setter, Frederick W.	41382	1915	45457	1920	
Setter, James H.	35741	1907	39615	1912	*[6]
Shapter, Joseph	20082	1877	21729	1882	*[7]
Shooter, Frank	19165	1873	19503	1874	
			20230	1877	2nd Clasp
			22058	1883	3rd Clasp
			22472	1884	4th Clasp
Slaughter, Frank	25602	1891	27711	1895	
			30829	1900	2nd Clasp
Smith, Charles Henry	22274	1884	22703	1885	
			23373	1887	2nd Clasp
Smith, Henry G.	21964	1883	23361	1886	
Smith, Richard	18801	1871	25954	1892	
Spinner, Charles	20592	1879	29256	1897	
Stark, Frederick	33630	1904	35846	1908	
Startin, James	19895	1879	22095	1883	*[8]
			32509	1903	2nd Clasp
Streader, William T.	17271	1864	19560	1875	*[9]
Sullivan, Timothy John	25349	1891	25743	1892	

			25897	1892	2nd Clasp
Swan, Stewart F.	39790	1913	41537	1915	
Taylor, Joseph G.	36809	1909	39279	1912	
Touhey, William	43399	1917	43526	1917	
Trafford, William Leigh	27528	1895	29006	1897	
Tremayne, George	35140	1907	37318	1910	
Turner, Henry C.	23652	1887	24794	1890	
Vaughan, John Owen	23204	1886	23668	1887	
Vaughan-Jones, Hubert	33489	1904	37048	1909	
Vingoe, Alfred	22631	1885	23660	1887	
Wackerell, George William	26068	1892	28217	1896	
Waters, Michael	23072	1886	24251	1889	*[10]
			25372	1891	2nd Clasp
Watkins, Milson	26623	1893	35791	1908	
Watson, John	27450	1894	29787	1898	
			41276	1914	2nd Clasp
			41280	1914	3rd Clasp
			45187	1919	4th Clasp
Watts, Henry	18244	1868	25844	1892	
Wenlock, Walter B.	36234	1908	42411	1916	
West, Daniel	24782	1890	53735	1936	
Whyte, Charles	18347	1869	22635	1885	
Williams, James	18256	1868	18479	1870	
Woods, Henry Byron	17979	1867	23272	1886	
Wray, George H.	18342	1869	19185	1873	
Wright, Walter John	22272	1884	23126	1886	
Young, Charles E.	27826	1895	38179	1911	
Young, Henry L.	18473	1870	18735	1871	

Analysis of Clasps

	Medals	Clasps
Medals with one clasp	189	189
Medals with two clasps	13	26
Medals with three clasps	4	12
Medals with four clasps	4	16
Medal with five clasps	1	5
Total	**201**	**248**

Notes:
*[1] W.D.Andrews — See 'Canadian Hero', LSARS Journal No.10 p.54
*[2] William Bradley — See 'A Southend Hero', LSARS Journal No.13 p.60
*[3] Hugh W.L.Holt — Also received Silver Medal (Case No.20446 - 1876)
*[4] James Jappy — 2nd & 3rd Clasps received for two life saving incidents both reported as Case No.41455
*[5] John Quince — Changed his name to Quinn
*[6] Joseph Shapter — Also received Silver Medal (Case No.23350 - 1886)
*[7] Frank Shooter — Also received Silver Medal (Case No.22473 - 1884). See 'Frank Shooter: Hero of the Exe', LSARS Journal No. 32 pp. 22-28.

*[8] James Startin   Also received Silver Medal (Case No.22537 - 1884)
*[9] Wm.T.Streader   Also received Silver Medal (Case No.17906 - 1867)
                      & Silver Clasp (Case No.18389 - 1869)
*[10] Michael Waters Also received Silver Medal (Case No.24051 - 1888)
                      & Silver Clasp (Case No.25204 - 1890)

Adams, William　　　　　　　　　　Medal　　　　　　　　　　　　　　　　25160

William Adams, at great personal risk, rescued R.Drane from drowning at Gorleston, on the 11th September 1890.

　　　　　　　　　　　　　　　　　Clasp　　　　　　　　　　　　　　　　29729-31

On 31st August 1898, a man was swept away while bathing at Gorleston. William Adams swam out and effected his rescue.

On the 14th September 1898, Charles Millar was bathing in 11 feet of water at Gorleston, and could not regain land. William Adams swam out and saved him.

On the 17th September 1898, two youths were carried out by the tide while bathing at Gorleston. William Adams swam out and, at great risk, took both to shore, but one of them was dead when landed.

　　　　　　　　　　　　　　　　　Clasp　　　　　　　　　　　　　　　　30217

On the 30th July 1899, a lady and gentleman were in a boat which they allowed to drift into the breakers at Gorleston. William Adams, at great risk, swam out, and having got into the boat rowed them to a place of safety.

　　　　　　　　　　　　　　　　　Clasp　　　　　　　　　　　　　　　　30791

On the 23rd July 1900, Henry Brown, while bathing in the sea at Gorleston, was seized with cramp and swept out 100 yards from shore. W.T.Sievey attempted to save him, but failed. At great risk, William Adams swam out and succeeded in saving him.

Testimonial on vellum to Sievey.

Alder, William N.　　　　　　　　　Medal　　　　　　　　　　　　　　　　43058

At 12.30 pm, on the 22nd November 1916, a man in trying to board his ship fell into the harbour at Sunderland; a second man went in, but was unable to help him, and also got into danger. William Alder, a pilot, went in with a rope and supported both men until further help came and they were got out.

　　　　　　　　　　　　　　　　　Clasp　　　　　　　　　　　　　　　　45037

At 4 pm, on the 18th August 1919, a boy fell into the River Wear from the North Pier, Sunderland. He was five yards from the pier and a depth of 8 feet when William N.Alder, pilot, jumped in and caught him and L.Robson, pilot, went down a rope and helped to hold him till a boat came.

Allistone, John　　　　　　　　　　Medal　　　　　　　　　　　　　　　　25104

John Allistone, postman, at great personal risk, rescued Thomas Fletcher from drowning in the Thames, at Twickenham, on the 7th September 1890.

　　　　　　　　　　　　　　　　　Clasp　　　　　　　　　　　　　　　　31073

On the 17th June 1900, a boy named Davis fell into the Lock Cut at Teddington. He had gone under water, when John Allistone, postman, at great risk, jumped in, and diving, was able to effect his rescue.

Pecuniary award also to Allistone.

Andrews, W.D. Medal 21420

W.D.Andrews, at great personal risk, rescued two persons from drowning at Toronto, Canada, on the 29th July 1881.

Clasp 21823

Captain W.D.Andrews, at great personal risk, rescued John Patey from drowning at Wyman's Island, Toronto, on the 25th September 1882.

Clasp 22181

Captain William Ward, Captain W.D.Andrews and John D.Patry, at great personal risk, rescued D.Schlockow from drowning in Toronto Bay during a great storm, on the 27th July 1883.

Silver Clasp to Ward; Bronze Medal to Patry.

Bamber, Walter Leigh Medal 17279

Mr W.L.Bamber, midshipman, HMS *Tribune*, jumped overboard and rescued Mr J.B.Johnson, master, same ship, at Calas, on the 31st May 1863. On 31st December 1863, he jumped overboard and rescued William Martin, also of HMS *Tribune*, at San Jose De Gualemata.

Clasp 18600

On the 22nd July 1870, at the Victory Pier, Jersey, Lieutenant W.L.Bamber, R.N., jumped overboard and rescued two men.

Barrett, Richard Medal 27323

Richard Barrett, at great personal risk, rescued two girls from drowning at Roundstone Bay, Co. Galway, 16th July 1894.

Clasp 36559

On the 21st March 1909. a youth fell into the sea from the landing stage at Margate and was carried out 100 yards by the tide. Richard Barrett swam out and managed to bring him back to the stage.

Barry, Michael Medal 42139

At 3.45 pm, on the 18th January 1917, an old man when unmooring a boat fell into the sea at Innismurry Island, Sligo, the depth being 40 feet and the sea choppy. Michael Barry, Constable, R.I.C., jumped in and caught him, and he was got into a boat.

Clasp 43653

At 1 pm, on the 1st August 1917, two girls were bathing in the sea at Mullaghmore and got into difficulty, one being carried 30 yards out and the other 80 yards. Michael Barry, Constable, R.I.C., went in and brought them to shore one at a time.

Beadle, Robert Graham Medal 26858

Robert Graham Beadle, ship's apprentice, at great personnel risk, rescued John Close from drowning at Sunderland, on the 6th September 1893.

Clasp 33043

At 1.30 am, on the 24th July 1903, the second engineer of the SS *Daghestan*, fell into the harbour at New York, the depth being 35 feet and the night dark. At great risk, R.G.Beadle, second officer of the ship, jumped in and succeeded in saving him.

Bear, Thomas Walter   Medal   24701

Thomas Walter Bear, lockman, at great personal risk, rescued John Sneath from drowning in the Albert Docks, London, E., on the 18th October 1889.

         Clasp   30576

On the 18th April 1900, T.W.Granger, while at play, fell into the Thames at North Woolwich, and there being a strong tide running he was soon carried out 20 yards from the bank. Thomas Walter Bear, pierman, sprang in and, at great risk, succeeded in landing him in safety.

Bell, Richard R.G.   Medal   29036

Richard A.Richards, Richard Bell and Thomas Jones, at great personal risk, rescued a girl from drowning at Aberdovey, North Wales, on the 21st August 1897.

Bronze Medals also to Richards and Jones.

         Clasp   40115

At 10 am, on the 23rd July 1913, F.Noble, while bathing in the sea at Aberdovey, got into difficulty 60 yards from shore in deep water. Richard R.G.Bell swam out from shore and kept him afloat till they were picked up by a boat.

Beresford, Lord Charles Wm. De La Poer

         Medal   17182

On the 18th September 1863, at Liverpool, Mr Richardson accidentally fell into the river. Lord Beresford jumped overboard and supported him in the water, where there was a strong current running, until saved by a boat hook. Richardson was exhausted.

         Clasp   18722

At 10 pm, on the 24th February 1871, at Port Stanley, Falkland Islands, William James, R.M.L.I., of HMS *Galatea*, fell into six fathoms of water. Lieutenant Lord C.Beresford, R.N. jumped overboard with heavy shooting clothes on and pockets filled with gun cartridges. John Harry, ship's corporal, jumped in and assisted to support the man until a boat arrived.

Berry, Ernest Reginald   Medal   53538

At 8 pm, on the 8th August 1936, at Croyde Bay, North Devon, F.H.Fischer (27), a citizen of Austria, and a friend were bathing and got into difficulties and were swept out. At the time the sea was rough and the beach dangerous. Ernest R.Berry (19), a clerk of Barnstaple, Devon, ran 200 yards and dived in and swam out 100 yards, depth eight feet, and brought Fischer out. Being told there was another, he also brought him in from shallow water. Restoration failed in this case.

         Clasp   53623

At 5.30 pm, on the 15th August 1936, in Croyde Bay, Devon, Miss Unity Perves was bathing and was carried out of her depth by the current, and in difficulties. Her cousin, also bathing, tried to support her. Ernest Reginald Berry (19), Clerk, Barnstaple, ran down the beach, swam out 75 yards to the girl, depth 6 to 10 feet, and swam with her a dozen strokes, when he could touch bottom. A friend brought a lifeline, to which he tied the girl and she was hauled out.

Beveridge, Alexander   Medal   18046

On 4th April 1867, at Constant Bay, New Zealand, Mr Alexander Beveridge went out through the surf with a life line and saved 13 of the crew of the steamer *Southland*.

         Clasp   18482

On the 15th October 1869, at Constant Bay, New Zealand, Captain A.Beveridge jumped from the rocks into the surf, and assisted four persons until the life boat arrived.

Blackmore, M.H.   Medal   34548

At 9.33 pm, on the 28th April 1906, a woman, in an attempt at suicide, threw herself into the Thames near Blackfriars Bridge. The night was dark and cold, the depth being eight feet with an ebb tide. At great risk, M.H.Blackmore, constable, City Police, plunged in and swam with her 70 to 80 yards, when they were picked up by a boat. John McGregor, a newsvendor, also jumped in, but his help was not required.

Pecuniary award to McGregor.

         Clasp   34692

At 9 pm, on the 26th June 1906, two boys were paddling in the Thames under Blackfriars Bridge, and getting out of their depth were soon in 16 feet of water, the place being very dangerous. M.H.Blackmore, City Police, at great risk, plunged in and succeeded in saving one, the other being drowned.

Blake, Stephen   Medal   18706

At 3.45 pm, on 2nd April 1871, Stephen Blake the lock keeper at Sandford Lock on the River Thames near Oxford, jumped into seven feet of water in the lock, and supported Sophia Wood until assistance arrived.

         Clasp   22788

Stephen Blake, lock-keeper, at great personal risk, rescued Kate Howse from drowning in the River Thames at Sandford, on the 21st July 1885.

Bolt, John   Medal   21844

J.Bolt, boatman Coastguard, at great personal risk, rescued two boys from drowning in the New Harbour, Torquay, on the 4th October 1882.

         Clasp   22456

John Bolt, boatman coastguard, at great personal risk, rescued John Brock from drowning at Weymouth, on the 16th August 1884.

Bone, John J.   Medal   18265

At 4 pm, on the 18th June 1868, at Grove Ferry, Canterbury, Kent, John Bone plunged into the water and extricated John Wilding from the weeds.

         Clasp   18941

At 6.30 am, on the 17th June 1872, at Messinger's Island, Surbiton, John J.Bone, stock broker, swam with his clothes on and brought R.Mothersill out, depth seven feet.

Booth, Arthur C.   Medal   37094

At 10 pm, on the 11th October 1909, a man in an attempt at suicide, threw himself into the Mersey at Liverpool. Arthur C.Booth, Customs Officer, jumped in from the launch and was successful in saving him.

         Clasp   42945

At 3.45 pm, on the 9th September 1916, a boy was washed from the slope of the pier into the Humber at Hull and was carried out about 20 yards. Arthur C.Booth, Customs Officer, plunged in and rescued him.

Bowen, Henry   Medal   25821

Henry Bow(e)n and James Welch, privates, 2nd Battalion Northumberland Fusiliers, at great personal risk, attempted to rescue Private G.Jefferson from drowning in Cabul River, Punjab, on the 11th April 1892.

Bronze Medal also to Welch.

                                    Clasp   29682

On the 22nd July 1898, Private Tyler, 15th Hussars, fell from his horse while practising swimming in the pond at Aldershot. Lieutenant Courage went to his assistance, but was clutched and in danger himself. Lieutenant Bald and Private Bowen then went in and rescued Tyler, while Lieutenant O.B.Walker plunged in and saved Courage.

Testimonial on vellum to Courage, Bald and Walker.

Bradley, William   Medal   21705

W.Bradley, light keeper, at great personal risk, rescued a boy from drowning at Southend on the 17th July 1882.

                                    Clasp   22089

William Bradley, at great personal risk, rescued Florence Hawkins from drowning at the Pier Head, Southend, on the 29th July 1883.

                                    Clasp   23977

William Bradley, pier-head keeper, at great personal risk, rescued a lad named Hanger from drowning at Southend, on the 3rd June 1888.

Brinkworth, George   Medal   23455

George Brinkworth, at great personal risk, rescued James Pritchard from drowning in a water tank at Cardiff, on the 30th April 1887.

                                    Clasp   39936

At 6.45 pm, on the 2nd June 1913, Robert Moon fell from a bridge into the Taff at Cardiff, the depth being 12 feet. George Brinkworth jumped in from a yacht and swam with him to a mud bank in mid river whence they were taken by a boat.

Bromley, Arthur   Medal   32512

On the 1st March 1903, a man of the R.M.A. accidentally fell into the sea at Weymouth. Lieutenant A.Bromley, HMS *Good Hope*, at once jumped in, and was able to rescue him.

                                    Clasp   35712

On the 10th October 1907, Thomas Smith fell into the sea from the South Parade Pier at Southsea, the sea being very rough with baulks of floating timber. Lieutenant A.Bromley, HM Yacht *Victoria and Albert*, and L.Richardson, coastguardsman, went in, but were unable to save him and he was drowned.

Bronze Medal to Richardson.

Brookes, G.C.   Medal   19662

At 11.40 am, on the 26th July 1875, N.Scolop fell into the River Thames at Westminster, depth of water being 9 feet. G.C.Brookes, 2nd Officer, P&O Company, jumped overboard with all his clothes on, dived for the man, and supported him until assisted on board the steamboat.

                                    Clasp   20748

On the 12th September 1879, at Woosung, a Lascar fell into the water. G.C.Brookes, 2nd Officer, P&O SS *Kaiser-i-Hind*, jumped overboard, dived twice and swam with the man to the tender.

Brown, William T. Medal 42263

At 9.30 pm, on the 21st January 1916, a woman threw herself from the Suspension Bridge into the Clyde at Glasgow, the night being dark and the river in flood. W.T.Brown, PC, swam out from the bank and succeeded in saving her.

Clasp 46216

At 9 pm, on the 10th November 1921, a woman named Agnes W.Weir, in attempting suicide, threw herself from the Suspension Bridge into the Clyde, 45 yards out and a depth of 15 feet, it being very cold. Detective Sergeant William T.Brown (34), Glasgow Police, threw off his jacket and vest and swam out and brought her to land.

Brunnen, James Medal 17985

On 20th May 1867, James Brunnen, captain's coxswain, HMS *Aurora*, jumped from Commissioners' Wharf, Quebec into the water and saved James Trescott of HMS *Aurora*.

Clasp 24868

James Brunnen, naval pensioner, at great personal risk, rescued Amelia Robinson, from drowning at Stokes Bay, on the 22nd May 1890.

Bryce (Brice), John Vincent Medal 24283

John Vincent Bryce, wharfinger, at great personal risk, rescued Francis Smith from drowning at Port Antonio, Jamaica, on the 27th July 1888.

Clasp 24768

James Vincent Brice, wharfinger, at great personal risk, rescued R.N.Knight from drowning at Port Antonio, Jamaica, on the 1st November 1889.

Buchan, Arthur (Andrew) G. Medal 38083

At 2.45 pm, on the 19th April 1911, two boys named McPherson were on the rocks at the South Bay, Peterhead, watching the surf, when both were swept off, the elder being carried out some distance. Arthur Buchan and George Buchan went in, Arthur saving the elder lad and George the younger.

Testimonial on vellum to G.Buchan.

Clasp 39493

At 1.30 pm, on the 6th September 1912, Alexander Third was washed overboard from a fishing boat some 30 miles E. by S. of Peterhead, there being a heavy sea with a gale blowing. Andrew G.Buchan, with a light line, went after him and succeeded in saving him.

Bull, John Medal 18289

At 5.30 pm, on the 18th July 1869, whilst at sea in the Gulf of Aden, George Young, ordinary seaman, HMS *Daphne*, fell overboard. Mr Charles E.Stuart, Midshipman, R.N. and John Bull, krooman, both jumped overboard, and Bull held the man up until rescued by the boat.

Clasp 18304

At 3.15 pm, on the 21st February 1869, Thomas Gardner, AB, fell overboard. John Bull, Krooman, HMS *Lynx*, jumped overboard, and was some time in the water; sharks were seen nearby.

Burke, Henry F.   Medal   26352

Henry F. Burke, potman, at great personal risk, rescued Albert Shepherd from drowning in the Thames, at Shadwell, on the 4th April 1893.

                                          Clasp   27833

Henry Burke, at great personal risk, rescued J. Nicholas from drowning in the Thames at Wapping, on the 28th June 1895.

Butters, Rev. William Middleton   Medal   21783

The Rev. W.M. Butters, at great personal risk, rescued a boy from drowning in the Seine, Paris, on the 12th August 1882.

                                          Clasp   22817

The Rev. William Middleton Butters, at great personal risk, rescued Peter Pizet from drowning at Guernsey, on the 31st July 1885.

Byrne, Henry   Medal   29229

Henry Byrne, fireman, at great personal risk, rescued John Leeson from drowning in the Liffey at Dublin, on the 11th October 1897.

                                          Clasp   29254

Henry Byrne, fireman, at great personal risk, rescued J. Murphy from drowning in the Liffey at Dublin, on the 7th November 1897.

Campbell, Duncan   Medal   31204

On the 9th April 1901, a boy named McCormick, accidentally fell into the river at Oban. At great risk, Duncan Campbell, joiner, sprang in and, with considerable difficulty, was able to effect the rescue.

                                          Clasp   31450

On the 20th July 1901, James M'Pherson, aged 60, fell from the North Pier into the sea at Oban, the depth being 18 feet. At great risk, Duncan Campbell, joiner, jumped in and supported him till they were picked up by a boat.

Carpendale, Trevor M.   Medal   43338

At 2.30 pm, on the 15th March 1917, two nurses were thrown into the Tigris owing to a collision between two boats, the depth being 20 feet with a strong current. Captain T.M. Carpendale, Indian Army, jumped in with a lifebuoy and kept them afloat until a tug picked them up.

                                          Clasp   55204

At noon, on the 13th November 1938, at Imli Kheria Jheel, Indore, a shikari, named Sepoy Ahmed Noor, swam out to retrieve a shot snipe, and became entangled in the thick weed and was in difficulties. Lieutenant Colonel Trevor M. Carpendale (53), Indian Army (Retd.), swam out 40 yards to his aid and got caught in the weeds and had difficulty in getting clear. Captain Roy D. Metcalfe (29), Indian Army, ran to the spot, dived in, swam across weed and dragged the man clear, and with Carpendale's help got him out.

Bronze Medal to Metcalfe.

Carr, John James Medal 30684

On the 31st May 1900, W.Gallagher, in an attempt at suicide, threw himself into the Tyne at Gateshead, there being a strong ebb tide, and the depth 12 to 14 feet. At great risk, John J.Carr, fireman, jumped in from a boat, and having caught him, they were picked up some distance down the river.

Clasp 30801

On the 30th July 1900, a lad named Banks, while at play, fell from the quay into the Tyne at Newcastle. At great risk, John J.Carr, labourer, jumped in, caught the lad, and landed him at the steps.

Clasp 32150

On the 10th August 1902, a boy named Anderson, while at play, fell into 18 feet of water in the Tyne at Newcastle. At great risk, John J.Carr jumped in, fully clothed, caught the lad, and swam with him to the landing. This is the 27th life saved by Carr.

Clasp 33297

On the 2nd July 1904, William Carr accidentally fell into the Tyne at Newcastle, the depth being 16 feet with a strong ebb tide. At great risk, John James Carr, labourer, jumped in and was successful in saving him.

Clasp 39009

At 6.30 pm, on the 23rd April 1912, P.Stevenson fell into the Tyne at Newcastle, the depth being 27 feet with a strong flood tide. John J.Carr at once plunged in fully clothed and succeeded in saving him.

Carruthers, John T. Medal 27983

J.T.Carruthers, Tyne River Police, at great personal risk, rescued R.Smith from drowning at South Shields, on the 22nd August 1895.

Clasp 34588

On the 8th May 1906, a boy fell from a boat into the Tyne at South Shields, there being a depth of 12 to 15 feet and a strong tide running. John T.Carruthers, constable, River Tyne Police, at great risk, jumped in and kept him afloat till they were picked up by a boat.

Cavill, Frederick Medal 18259

At 9.30 am, on the 1st September 1868, at Brighton, Sussex, Frederick Cavill ran to the beach, jumped into the sea with his clothes on, swam to George Henry Jupp, depth 20 feet, and brought him ashore.

Clasp 18641

At 1.15 pm, on the 1st September 1870, Frederick Cavill swam out from the beach at Brighton, Sussex, with all his clothes on, and brought Mrs M.Simmonds ashore.

Ceil(e)y, George R. Medal 21810

G.R.Ceiley, bandsman, R.A., at great personal risk, rescued a woman from drowning at Lowestoft on the 5th August, and again on the 20th August 1882, rescued a boy who had fallen from a steamer into the River Yare, Great Yarmouth.

Clasp 25635

Harry J. Isaacs and George R.Ceily, at great personal risk, rescued a gentleman from drowning at Great Yarmouth, on the 30th August 1891.

Bronze Clasp to Isaacs.

Channer, George K. Medal 27280

George K.Channer, at great personal risk, rescued H.C.Lloyd from drowning at Eastbourne, 18th August 1894.

Clasp 31300

On the 20th May 1901, a native boatman fell from his boat into the lake at Naukatchiee, India. At great risk, Lieutenant G.K.Channer, 3rd Ghurka Rifles, went after him, but being clutched had a hard struggle to keep him afloat till they were picked up by another boat.

Channon, Samuel Medal 18167

At 8.30 pm, on the 25th June 1868, at Barnstaple, Devon, Samuel Channon jumped from a boat, swam to Samuel Camp, and supported him until rescued by a boat.

Clasp 19427

At 2 pm, on the 9th July 1874, in the River Taw at Blackrock, Barnstaple, Samuel Channon swam out to Sidney Richards, tailor, depth eight feet, and brought the lad ashore.

Churchill, William Medal 18398

At noon, on the 3rd September 1869, Charles Pelham fell into the River Arun at Littlehampton-by-Sea, depth ten feet. William Churchill jumped in with all his clothes on, dived, and brought the child out.

Clasp 18792

At 7.30 am, on the 29th July 1871, Edward de Grave-Sells, fell into the River Arun at Littlehampton, Sussex, depth 16 feet. William Churchill, boatman, jumped into the river, swam 30 or 40 yards with the child to the side of the pier.

Clowes, Alfred Medal 33164

On the 16th April 1904, a boy named Worthington fell into the Lune at Lancaster and was carried 25 yards out into a depth of 12 feet. Alfred Clowes, licensed victualler, jumped in, and after a swim of 60 yards got him out in an unconscious state, from which R.Bleasdale successfully restored him.

Certificate to Bleasdale.

Clasp 34785

On the 26th July 1906, a boy fell from the quay into the Lune at Lancaster, the depth being 18 to 20 feet, with a strong tide running. At great risk, Alfred Clowes jumped in, fully clothed, and succeeded in swimming with him to a boat.

Coleman, Albert E. Medal 21169

At 5.30pm, on 30th November 1880, A.E.Coleman, AB, of HMS *Valiant*, plunged overboard into the River Shannon and with great difficulty supported T.Berry, captain of the maintop, until assistance arrived.

Clasp 21966

Lieutenant Kepple Wade, RN, and Albert E.Coleman, AB, HMS *Achilles*, at great personal risk, rescued W.Peacock from drowning at sea, on the 23rd April 1883.

Bronze Medal to Wade.

Clasp 22989

Albert E.Coleman, captain of the foretop, and John Hewitt, AB, of HMS *Bellerophon*, at great personal risk, saved two seamen from drowning in Plymouth Sound, on the 13th January 1886.

Bronze Medal to Hewitt.

Congdon, George T. Medal 22935

George T.Congdon, AB, and James A.Hadley, leading seaman, HMS *Excellent*, at great personal risk, rescued Trooper James McGarry from drowning in Langston Harbour, on the 29th September 1885.

Bronze Medal to Hadley.

Clasp 28723

G.Congdon, petty officer, and Henry Cosh, leading seaman of HMS *Hero*, at great personal risk, rescued J.Newman from drowning at Portsmouth, on the 27th February 1897.

Bronze Medal to Cosh.

Cook, David E. Medal 22211

David E.Cook, at great personal risk, saved A.Mitchels from drowning in the Fish Dock, Lowestoft, on the 5th December 1883.

Clasp 23257

David E.Cook, bathing attendant, at great personal risk, rescued two ladies from drowning at Lowestoft, on the 26th August 1886.

Clasp 23369

David E.Cook, bathing machine proprietor, at great personal risk, rescued Samuel C.Shenfield from drowning at Lowestoft, on the 8th December 1886.

Clasp 26253

David Cook, fisherman, at great personal risk, rescued Herbert Norman from drowning at Lowestoft, on the 10th December 1892.

Cosh, Henry Medal 28723

G.Congdon, petty officer, and Henry Cosh, leading seaman of HMS *Hero*, at great personal risk, rescued J.Newman from drowning at Portsmouth, on the 27th February 1897.

Bronze Clasp to Congdon.

Clasp 34758

On the 18th July 1906, Ernest A.Brown, AB, was thrown into the sea at Lundy Island, owing to a sling giving way. Henry Cosh, Petty Officer 1st class, HMS *Duncan*, at great personal risk, plunged in and succeeded in saving him.

Craig, George Medal 26947

George Craig and James Craig, assisted by James Craig, senior, rescued Joseph Dixon from drowning at Newcastle-on-Tyne, 15th January 1894.

Bronze Medal to James Craig.

Clasp 27401

George Craig, at great personal risk, attempted to rescue two men from drowning in the Tyne at Newcastle, 2nd October 1894.

Clasp 31067

On the 16th November 1900, a woman named Jane Clift, in an attempt at suicide, threw herself into the Tyne at Newcastle. The depth at the time was some 17 feet. At great risk, George Craig jumped in from a height of 20 feet, caught the woman, and succeeded in saving her, after which J.H.Walton used means for her restoration.

Certificate to Walton.

Craner, Edward Medal 19204

At 8 pm, on the 28th July 1873, John Halliday of Bow, fell into the River Thames at Bankside, Southwark, the depth being eight feet. Edward Craner (19), jumped into the river, swam to the spot where the boy went down, dived three times, and succeeded in bringing him ashore. He was taken to the 'Welsh Trooper', Bankside where he recovered.

£1 pecuniary award to landlord.

Clasp 20197

At 6 pm, on the 29th July 1877, J.Naylor fell into the River Thames at East Molesey, the depth being 12 feet. E.Craner jumped into the water with all his clothes on, dived, and brought the boy to shore.

Crichton, James Medal and Clasp 18800

At 8.45 pm, on the 30th July 1871, a man fell into the Victoria Docks at Leith and James Crichton, lithographic printer plunged in and brought the man to shore. At 6.45 am on the 4th August 1871, John McNeill fell from the Chain Pier at Trinity into 19 feet of water and James Crichton again plunged in and brought the man ashore.

Cruttenden, Frank Percy Medal 61366

On the 23rd February 1950, two boys, Roy Rutherford (12) and Keith Hemfrey (9), both of Dr. Barnardos Homes, got lost walking along the foreshore at Fairlight Glen, near Hastings. The Hastings Police were told of their absence and they asked the Coastguards to help. Coastguards with the Life Saving Company went to the cliff top, arriving about midnight. The foreshore covers at high water and it was three hours off high water so speed was essential. The Station Officer split his party into three groups. Normally the cliffs can be descended by experienced climbers without cliff ropes but this was not so easy in the dark. Each party sat down and eased themselves down the cliff in easy stages. At the foot of the cliffs at Fairlight Glen there is a cordoned off minefield and after searching in the dark the boys were found within this area. Frank Percy Cruttenden (49), coastguard, and Edward Henry Brazier (34), coastguard, entered the minefield and got the boys out. The ascent was worse than the descent the party going up on hands and knees carrying the boys.

Bronze Medal to Brazier.

Clasp 61498

On the 18th June 1950 Eric Raymond Key (22), french polisher, and a friend were visiting Hastings for the day and decided to climb the cliffs at Ecclesbourne Glen, from the beach to the top. When about 30 feet from the top Key became trapped and could not move in any direction. The other man had abandoned the climb. The Police and Coastguards were called. Ernest Charles Cooke (40), auxiliary coastguard, in a slung position on the cliff intercepted signals by Frank Percy Cruttenden (49), coastguard, and facilitated the rescue. This was a dangerous rescue owing to the crumbling nature of the cliff. Both men were recommended equally.

Bronze Medal to Cooke.

Curtis, Thomas E. Medal 22523

Thomas E.Curtis, at great personal risk, rescued C.E.Burls from drowning in the River Thames, at Tilbury, on the 20th September 1884.

Clasp 23445

Thomas E.Curtis, 2nd mate, at great personal risk, rescued William Warren from drowning in the Thames at Blackwall, on the 1st April 1887.

Dacres, Seymour Henry Pelham Medal 17510

On the 2nd July 1865, near Portland Harbour, Mr S.H.P.Dacres, midshipman, HMS *Black Prince*, jumped overboard with a life buoy and rescued a boy from the same ship.

Clasp 19632

At 4.07 am, on the 14th May 1875, in the Atlantic Ocean, lat.10^0 15'N., long.21^0 39'W., William Duncanson, AB, fell overboard from HMS *Newcastle*. Lieutenant E.S.Poë jumped overboard from the hammock nettings, swam to the man, and supported him to a life buoy. Commander S.H.P.Dacres jumped out of his cabin port, swam to the man, and aided in supporting him to the life buoy.

Bronze Medal to Lieutenant Poë.

Davis, Frederick J. Medal 21620

F.J.Davis, 4th Officer of the SS *Rome*, at great personal risk, rescued a Lascar from drowning in the Royal Albert Dock, London, on the 15th May 1882.

Clasp 22382

Frederick J.Davis, 2nd Officer, P&O steamer *Poonah*, rescued W.H.Pring from drowning in the Albert Docks, on the 15th July 1884.

Davis, Snowden Medal 22919

Snowden Davis, apprentice, at great personal risk, rescued William Taylor from drowning in the River Tyne, at Redheugh Bridge, on the 23rd September 1885.

Clasp 23438

Snowden Davis, plater, at great personal risk, rescued James Harrrison from drowning in the River Tyne, at Newcastle, on the 25th March 1887.

Donohue, Daniel Medal 18870

At 2 pm, on the 19th January 1871 at Gibraltar, Henry Devonshire, ordinary seaman, fell overboard from HMS *Sultan* into 15 fathoms of water. Daniel Donohue, boatswain, and George Slimme, leading seaman, HMS *Sultan*, both jumped overboard from the knight-heads (sic), a height of 22 feet, with a heavy sea and strong breeze, and helped get him on board the cutter.

Bronze Medal to Slimme.

Clasp 19652

At 7.30, on the 5th July 1875, at Arosa Bay, Thomas Atwood, Ordinary seaman, HMS *Sultan*, fell overboard into nine fathoms of water. Daniel Donohue, boatswain, same ship, jumped overboard from the fore chains and swam with the man to the gangway of the ship.

Douglas, Henry Medal 17910

On the 22nd February 1867, Henry Douglas, pierman, jumped into the River Thames and rescued T.H.Banbury.

Clasp 21609

Henry Douglas, piermaster, Westminster, at great personal risk, assisted to rescue Louis Sholl from drowning in the Thames on the 22nd April 1882.

Drake, H.M.   Medal   9194

The Reverend H.M.Drake, at great personal risk, rescued a boy from drowning in the Torridge at Bideford, on the 28th August 1897.

                                    Clasp   29418

On the 5th June 1898, Gilbert Rendel fell from a wall into the Torridge at Bideford; there was a strong tide running, the depth being 16 feet. The Reverend H.M.Drake, Curate of Bideford, jumped in, and at great risk supported Rendel till they were picked up by a boat.

Drane, Robert   Medal   29807

On the 12th November 1898, a boy fell into the Tyne at Newcastle, the current carrying him under a floating raft. Robert Drane, fisherman, at great risk, plunged in, and diving succeeded in saving the lad.

                                    Clasp   30144

On the 10th July 1899, C.Thompson, a miner, fell from the quay into the Tyne at Newcastle, the depth at the time being 15 feet. Robert Drane, fisherman, jumped in and, at great risk, succeeded in saving him. This rescue brings Drane's record up to 50 lives saved.

                                    Clasp   31490

On the 24th July 1901, a woman in an attempt at suicide, threw herself into the Ouseburn at Newcastle. Robert Drane and Philip Renforth both went in but Renforth failed to save the woman, Drane then, at great risk, effected her rescue.

Testimonial on vellum to Renforth.

                                    Clasp   31805

On the 7th December 1901, a man fell from the quay into the Ouseburn at Newcastle, the depth being ten feet with a strong ebb tide. At great risk, Robert Drane, fisherman, jumped in from a height of 16 feet and succeeded in saving him.

                                    Clasp   36919

On the 14th August 1909, G.Heppel got into deep water while bathing in the Ouseburn at Newcastle. H.Coatsworth, aged 14, went in to his help, but also got into danger. Robert Drane then plunged in and rescued both lads.

Testimonial on vellum to Coatsworth.

Dryden, James   Medal   27636

James Dryden, at great personal risk, rescued Joseph Dixon from drowning in the Tyne, at Newcastle, on the 22nd April 1895.

                                    Clasp   29618

On the 6th August 1898, a woman, in an attempt to commit suicide, threw herself into the Tyne at Newcastle, the depth being 30 feet, with a strong tide running. James Dryden, labourer, sprang in from the quay, caught the woman, and took her to the side, where they were taken into a boat.

Dulon, Martin   Medal   23430

Martin Dulon, butler, at great personal risk, rescued James Stevens from drowning at St.Leonard's-on-Sea, on the 23rd March 1887.

                                    Clasp   24038

Martin Dulon, butler, at great personal risk, assisted in saving two gentlemen from drowning at St.Leonard's-on-Sea, on the 5th August 1888.

Dunbar, Herman Medal 42849

At 2 pm, on the 5th June 1916, a girl fell overboard from a steamer in the river at Georgetown, Demerara, the depth being 17 feet and danger from sharks. Herman Dunbar, sailor, jumped in from his ship and succeeded in saving her.

Clasp 46631

At 9 am, on the 6th August 1922, at Georgetown, Demerara, a man was in a boat which capsized and was being swept away by the tide, the depth being 17 feet and danger from sharks. Herman Dunbar, sailor, jumped overboard and succeeded in bringing him back to the ship where he was hauled on board.

Edwards, Albert Medal 37960

At 5.30 pm, on the 2nd December 1910, a man named Wheatcroft, in trying to pass through the flood caused by an overflow of the Derwent at Derby, was swept away, but managed to grasp a fence about 200 yards from the water's edge. A.Edwards went in, and tying a rope around him, he was dragged to land.

Clasp 38848

At 10 am, on the 23rd September 1911, Harold Harris, while swimming across the Vaal River at Parys, Orange River Colony, took cramp 25 yards from the side in a depth of 12 feet. Albert Edwards, sapper, R.E., plunged in and succeeded in saving him.

Ellard, Joseph Medal 24657

Joseph Ellard, railway clerk, at great personnel risk, rescued Alexander Leitch from drowning at the Station Pier, Loch Awe, on the 23rd August 1889.

Clasp 31620

On the 9th September 1901, a little girl fell into the canal lock at Ardrishaig, there being a great rush of water owing to the sluices being open. Joseph Ellard, purser on the SS *Linnet*, at great risk, jumped in and supported her till they were assisted to land.

Enderstein, Seigfred M. Medal and Clasp 40681

At 10.30 am, on the 14th March 1913, a boy of nine fell into the sea at Langebaan, Cape Colony. Seigfred M.Enderstein, aged 12, plunged in and rescued him. At 3 pm on the 31st October 1913, a girl fell into a depth of 15 feet and was being carried away by the tide. On this occasion also Enderstein went in and rescued her.

Falconer, Joseph Medal 23839

Joseph Falconer, shipwright, at great personal risk, rescued Charles Lloyd from drowning at East London, South Africa, on the 18th August 1887.

Clasp 28117

Joseph Falconer, W.Kinloch, A.Kinloch, and W.Anderson, at personal risk, rescued six men, being the master and crew of the ship *Avance*, which was wrecked at Garmouth, Moray Firth, on the 23rd October 1895.

Testimonials on vellum to W.Kinloch; on parchment to A.Kinloch and W.Anderson.

Fant, John Medal 51292

At 2.30 pm, on the 29th May 1932, at sea, Lat. 13°N., Long. 40°E., Hui So, a female Chinese passenger, fell overboard from the SS *Hin Sang*. Chief Officer J.Fant, same ship, dived in and held her till picked up by a boat.

Clasp 52568

At 9.50 am, on the 15th September 1934, in the South China Sea, Lat. 14° 45'N., Long.113° 28'E., a woman named Ho Fei Yin, on passage to Hong Kong jumped overboard. The ship's speed was 11_ knots, the wind SSE and the sea was shark infested. Chief Officer John Fant, SS *Kumsary*, dived in and swam out, but failed to find her. He was picked up 35 minutes later.

Ferguson, W. Medal 21479

W.Ferguson, at great personal risk, rescued a man from drowning at Liverpool, on the 10th August 1881.

Clasp 21540

W.Ferguson, of the SS *Emerald Isle*, at great personal risk, jumped overboard, and rescued H.J.Honeyford from drowning at Liverpool, on the 21st December 1881.

Fieldhouse, Walter Medal 18618

At 5.30 pm, on the 15th September 1870, at Barnard Castle, Durham, Walter Fieldhouse jumped with his clothes on into the River Tees, depth 16 feet, and brought a child, John Valence, to land.

Clasp 18686

At 2.15 pm, on the 5th February 1871, at Barnard Castle, Durham, Thomas Hodgson fell through the ice on the River Tees, depth 15 feet. Walter Fieldhouse and Richard Holmes, both went on the ice and became immersed, but succeeded in bringing the lad out.

Finnis, James W. Medal 34004

On the 10th July 1905, a woman in an attempt at suicide, threw herself into the Medway at Chatham, the distance from the landing being 80 yards and the depth 20 feet. At great risk, N.E.Gurton and J.W.Finnis, police constables, jumped in, and were successful in saving her.

Bronze Medal to Gurton.

Clasp 37922

At 10.45 pm, on the 1st November 1910, a woman, who had first cut her throat, threw herself into the dock entrance at Strood. James W.Finnis, police constable, plunged in and supported her till they were got out with a ladder.

Fippin(g), Ernest Medal 22551

Ernest Fipping, commissioned boatman, coastguard, at great personal risk, rescued Ernest E.Reep from drowning at Devonport, on the 30th July 1884.

Clasp 25068

Ernest Fippin, boatman, coastguard, at great personal risk, rescued George Mitchell from drowning at Sandhaven, New Brunswick, on the 29th July 1890.

Fisher, William Blake　　　　　　　　Medal　　　　　　　　　　　　　　21925

Lieutenant W.B.Fisher, R.N., and F.N.Rose, 1st class boy, HMS *St. Vincent*, at great personal risk rescued T.P.Hunt from drowning in Portsmouth Harbour, on the 10th February 1883.

　　　　　　　　　　　　　　　　　Clasp　　　　　　　　　　　　　　22655

Lieutenant W.B.Fisher, R.N., and Albert Giddings, 2nd captain of deck men, HMS *Miranda*, at great personal risk, saved A.E.Steele, AB, from drowning in Sydney Harbour, on the 3rd January 1885.

Bronze Medal to Giddings.

Fitch, Walter　　　　　　　　　　　Medal　　　　　　　　　　　　　　33186

On the 8th April 1904, Thomas Cove, aged 9, fell into the Regent's Canal, Hoxton, the depth of the place being 12 feet. Walter Fitch, schoolboy, aged 12, at great risk, jumped in, fully clothed, and rescued him.

　　　　　　　　　　　　　　　　　Clasp　　　　　　　　　　　　　　33735

On the 7th January 1905, Sydney Peck was pushed into the Regent's Canal, Hoxton, there being at the place a depth of eight feet. At great risk, W.Gardiner, aged 11, went in, but was dragged under water by Peck, when Walter Fitch, aged 13, jumped in and succeeded in rescuing both boys.

Testimonial on vellum to Gardiner.

Flemyng, Archibald E.F.　　　　　　Medal　　　　　　　　　　　　　　22132

Archibald E.Flemyng, at great personal risk, rescued two boys from drowning at St. Helena, on the 16th May 1883.

　　　　　　　　　　　　　　　　　Clasp　　　　　　　　　　　　　　27745

Captain A.E.F.Flemyng, Lieutenant, RNR, at great personal risk, was the means of rescuing several men, the crew of a capsized boat, in Lagos Bay, West Coast of Africa, in January 1895.

Foot(e), Thomas　　　　　　　　　Medal　　　　　　　　　　　　　16308(a)

On the 19th January 1859, Denis Ball (43), coal trimmer, of the steam ship *Tyne*, accidentally fell into the water in the Docks at Southampton. Thomas Foot, seaman, of the steam ship *Tamar*, jumped in with his clothes on and swam to the exhausted man and supported him till they were picked up by a boat.

　　　　　　　　　　　　　　　　　Clasp　　　　　　　　　　　　　　24048

Thomas Foote, at great personal risk, rescued Edward Hansford from drowning at Southampton, on the 18th July 1888.

Foster, George　　　　　　　　　Medal　　　　　　　　　　　　　　21428

Sergeant G.Foster, 1st Battalion, Gordon Highlanders, at great personal risk, rescued Private M.Phipps from drowning at Malta, on the 23rd July 1881. Surgeon-Major Riorden attended.

　　　　　　　　　　　　　　　　　Clasp　　　　　　　　　　　　　　23105

Sergeant George Foster, 1st Battalion, Gordon Highlanders, at great personal risk, rescued Margarita Carnana from drowning at Malta, on the 9th May 1886.

Freeland, Alfred   Medal   18998

At 5.15 pm, on the 26th April 1872, at Amery, China, John Hanlon, ordinary seaman, HMS *Rinaldo*, fell overboard into 12 fathoms of water. Alfred Freeland, 2nd captain maintop, same ship, jumped overboard, swam to the man, and brought him to the gangway of the ship.

                                            Clasp   19551

At night, on the 3rd November 1874, in the river at Shanghai, China, a seaman fell overboard from the United States SS *Hartford*. Alfred Freeland, 2nd captain of the forecastle, HMS *Dwarf*, jumped into the river and rescued the man.

Fullick, Edward   Medal   28036

Edward Fullick, at great personal risk, rescued, and Police Constable Campion attempted to rescue, Miss Newton from drowning at Surbiton on the 3rd September 1895.

Testimonial on parchment to Campion.

                                            Clasp   32456

On the 15th December 1902, a girl accidentally fell into the Thames at Kingston, there being a strong stream running and the weather very cold. Edward Fullick, lighterman, at great risk, jumped in from a tug and rescued her.

Gladding, George   Medal   32022

On the 27th June 1902, Sidney Coe accidentally fell into the Orwell at Ipswich, there being a depth of 15 to 20 feet. George Gladding, master of steam barge, plunged in and, after swimming 100 yards, caught the lad and took him to the bank.

                                            Clasp   33872

On the 1st June 1905, a man named Pritchard, whilst under the influence of drink, fell into the Orwell at Ipswich. At great risk, George Gladding went in, and succeeded in rescuing him.

Glasson, Thomas S.   Medal   28975

Thomas Glasson, clerk, at great personal risk, rescued G.Bossence from drowning in the Taw at Barnstaple, on the 22nd June 1897.

                                            Clasp   31099

On the 18th December 1900, J.S.Cook, stoker, HMS *Pelorus*, accidentally fell overboard in the Barnpool, Plymouth. There was a very strong ebb tide running and very dark at the time. Private T.S.Glasson, RMLI, jumped in from the ship, but was too late, as Cook sank before being reached.

Goldsmith, Henry   Medal   22271

Henry Goldsmith, at great personal risk, rescued Thomas Saint from drowning in the River Ouse, King's Lynn, on the 28th March 1884.

                                            Clasp   32336

On the 23rd July 1902, two boys, while fishing, fell into the Ouse at King's Lynn. There was a strong tide and the depth 15 feet. At great risk, Henry Goldsmith, bricklayer, jumped in, fully clothed, and saved them, one at a time.

Gonsalves, Manoel   Medal   46686

At 11.30 am, on the 31st December 1922, Miss Mary Salisbury (35) was bathing at Funchal, Madeira. She was unable to swim and got into difficulties and was being carried away by the backwash. Manoel Gonsalves, bathing attendant (25), went in and with some difficulty kept her up until the boat reached them.

Clasp   47648

At 1 pm, on the 10th January 1925, at Funchal, Madeira, Miss Roseanne Riley (19) was in the bathing pool and Miss Angela Pell (25) in the sea, when a huge tidal wave broke over the rock and took Miss Pell 30 yards out into five fathoms of water. Manoel Gonsalves, bathing attendant (30), first saved Miss Riley, then swam out and brought Miss Pell back to safety.

Gornall, Henry   Medal   16549

On the 5th July 1860, Samuel Lynn (15) sank while bathing in the River Tyne at Low Elswick. Henry Gornall swam to his assistance and succeeded in bringing him to shore in an insensible state.

Clasp   23426

Henry Gornall, traveller, at great personal risk, rescued Allon Jaques from drowning in a pond at Lemington, near Newcastle, on the 25th January 1887.

Grace, Edward   Medal   28695

Edward Grace, master mariner, at great personal risk, rescued George Welton from drowning in the Humber at Goole, on the 22nd January 1897.

Clasp   32898

On the 7th July 1903, a man named Lister, fell into the canal lock at Naburn, Yorkshire, there being a depth of 17 feet of water. Edward Grace, master mariner, ran some distance and, at great risk, plunged in, but after diving several times, was unable to find him.

Grant, Richard S.   Medal   35405

On the 13th July 1907, Henry W. White was thrown into the sea off Swanage owing to his yacht being run down by a steamer. Richard Grant, who was also on the yacht, swam to his help and supported him till they were picked up by a boat.

Clasp   38316

On the afternoon of the 5th July 1911, a boat was run down by a steamer in Swanage Bay, and one of the passengers, a woman, was in danger. Richard S. Grant, the boatman, swam to her help and kept her afloat till they were picked up.

Gray, H.C. Barton   Medal   20829

At 5.20 pm, on the 18th January 1880, Lieutenants R.C. Pentland and H.C. Barton Gray, 103rd Fusiliers, plunged into the River Lee, Cork, with their clothes on, and with great difficulty rescued C. Bateman, cattle drover.

Bronze Medal to Lieutenant Pentland.

Clasp   28222

Major H.C.B. Gray and S.A. Hawkes, 2nd Officer of the SS *Dilwara*, at great personal risk, rescued John Binder, AB, from drowning in the harbour at Bombay, on the 2nd January 1896.

Testimonial on vellum to Hawkes.

Gregory, Thomas R.   Medal   26593

Thomas Gregory, waterman, at great personal risk, rescued Robert Bond from drowning at Exeter, on the 5th July 1893.

                                   Clasp   30010

On the 28th May 1899, a boy fell into the harbour at Exeter in a very dangerous place, between a ship and the quay, the depth of water being ten feet. Thomas R.Gregory, boatman, at great risk, jumped down and rescued him.

Pecuniary award also to Gregory.

Griffiths, Thomas   Medal   16294

On the 13th April 1859, Thomas Warren accidentally fell into the River Parrett at Bridgewater, the depth being 12 feet and a strong tide running. Thomas Griffiths, pilot, jumped in with his clothes on, swam to the man's assistance and rescued him in an insensible state. Griffiths has saved 15 lives previously.

                                   Clasp   19683

At 6.30 pm, on the 1st August 1875, a boy named Thomas Knight fell into the River Parrett at Bridgewater, Somerset, the depth being 14 feet. Thomas Griffiths, pilot, jumped into the river, swam to the boy, and brought him out by the hair of his head.

Grunsell, W.H.   Medal   21521

W.H.Grunsell, AB, HMS *Minotaur*, at great personal risk, rescued W.J.Tonge, AB, of the same ship, from drowning in Bantry Bay, on the 4th November 1881.

                                   Clasp   30066

On the 17th June 1899, a child while at play fell into the Thames at Westminster. At great risk W.H.Grunsell, yachtsman, jumped in, swam with him under the bridge, and landed him.

Hammet, James Lacon   Medal   19581

At 4 pm, on the 26th February 1875 whilst at sea at the entrance of the English Channel on board HMS *Lord Warden*, Lieutenant J.L.Hammet, RN, and E.C.Jeffery, RN, acting Navigating Sub Lieutenant, both jumped overboard from the poop and supported boy 1st class, William Brears, until a boat arrived from the ship.

Bronze Medal to Jeffery.

                                   Clasp   22679

Captain James L.Hammet, RN, James Hardy, quartermaster, RN, and James Searle, AB, all of HMS *Agincourt*, saved T.Dunnavan from drowning near Roche Point, Queenstown, on the 13th April 1885.

Parchments to Hardy and Searle.

Hellyer, Edwin A.   Medal   28256

Edwin A.Hellyer, constable, River Tyne Police, at great personal risk, rescued J.W.Rochester from drowning in the mill dam gut, River Tyne, on the 19th April 1896.

                                   Clasp   29059

Constable E.A.Hellyer, River Tyne Police, at great personal risk, rescued C.F.McAllum from drowning at Tynemouth, on the 18th August 1897.

Henderson, Arnott　　　　　Medal　　　　　19527

At 6 pm, on the 25th August 1874, at San Jose de Quatemala, William Winn, ordinary seaman, fell into 12 feet of water. Herbert E.M.Bourke, midshipman, R.N., and Arnott Henderson, navigating midshipman, R.N., of HMS *Tenedos*, both jumped overboard, and brought the man to the ship's side; he was then hauled up by ropes, sharks having been seen in the harbour the same day.

Bronze Medal to Midshipman Bourke.

　　　　　Clasp　　　　　19630

At 5 pm, on the 26th January 1875 at Honolulu, Charles Wilson, A.B., fell into 4_ fathoms of water. Mr Arnott Henderson, navigating midshipman, R.N., HMS *Tenedos*, swam to the spot where the man went down and unsuccessfully tried to rescue him.

　　　　　Clasp　　　　　19778

At 6.30 am, on the 24th June 1875, in mid ocean, off the coast of Chile, J.M.Lloyd, Navigating Lieutenant, R.N., HMS *Tenedos*, fell overboard. John Walter Scott, Surgeon, R.N., and Navigating Lieutenant A.Henderson, R.N., same ship, both jumped overboard and supported him until they were picked up by a boat.

Bronze Medal to Mr Scott.

Herd, Robert　　　　　Medal　　　　　26014

Robert Herd, lock-keeper, at great personal risk, rescued Frederick Nash from drowning in the Thames at Osney Lock, on the 11th July 1892.

　　　　　Clasp　　　　　26607

Robert Herd, lock-keeper, at great personal risk, rescued Joseph Lee from drowning in the Thames, at Osney Lock, on the 16th July 1893.

Hodgson, Joseph R.　　　　　Medal　　　　　19052

At 3 pm, on the 12th October 1872, a boy named Thomas Daines, fell into the Regent's Canal Dock at Limehouse. J.R.Hodgson jumped into the water, swam with the boy to the piles, and supported him until a boat arrived.

　　　　　Clasp　　　　　20959

At 5.30 pm, on the 13th July 1880, a lad named J.Keohan, fell into the River Thames at Limehouse. J.Hodgson jumped into the river, dived after the lad, and rescued him.

Hollingsworth, E.　　　　　Medal　　　　　38249

At 10 am, on the 26th June 1911, J.H.Howarth was thrown into the sea at Spithead owing to Torpedo Boat *86* running down a cutter from HMS *Achilles*. E.Hollingsworth, AB, plunged in and rescued him.

　　　　　Clasp　　　　　39752

At 1.15 pm, on the 11th January 1913, a man fell from the boom ladder of HMS *Achilles* into the sea at Spithead. Lieutenant A.F.B.Carpenter, Herbert F.Bundy, AB, and E.Hollingworth, AB, went in and, between them, managed to save the man.

Bronze Medals to Lieutenant Carpenter and Bundy.

Holloway, Graham C.   Medal   33039

On the 10th July 1903, a Chinese coolie fell into the river at Shanghai, there being a very strong tide and the depth 28 feet. Graham C.Holloway, chief officer, P&O SS *Coromandel*, plunged in and kept him afloat till both were got out with a rope.

            Clasp   34287

On the 8th August 1905, L.W.Adkins fell overboard from the P&O tender off Woosung, China, it being dark at the time and a three knot tide running. G.C.Holloway, chief officer P&O SS *Coromandel*, at great risk, jumped in and supported him till they were picked up by a boat.

Holt, Hugh W.L.   Medal   17850

On the 13th July 1866, the barque *William Watson*, was wrecked off Newcastle, New South Wales. H.W.L.Holt swam through very heavy sea and surf and took a rope on board so the crew were saved.

            Clasp   19135

At 4.30 pm, on the 3rd October 1873 at Newcastle, New South Wales, a seaman of the SS *Grafton*, fell into 17 feet of water. Hugh W.L.Holt plunged into the water with clothes on and succeeded in landing the man.

Hood, James Samuel   Medal   19834

At 2.30 pm, on the 8th May 1876 on the River Thames at Poplar, James Hood slid down the rudder chain, jumped and caught hold of the tow rope, then hauled himself along under the water until he reached W.F. Fenwick, a lighterman of Bowen Street, London. He released Fenwick's leg from the rope, made for the skiff, and held on to him until assistance arrived.

            Clasp   22243

James Samuel Hood, at great personal risk, rescued Private James Shields from drowning in the River Thames, at Irongate Wharf, on the 6th February 1884.

Hooton, James W.   Medal   18348

At 8.20 pm, on the 11th July 1869, at Wisbeach, James W.Hooton jumped in with all his clothes on, and saved a child named James Hanstead, depth 20 feet.

            Clasp   18682

At 4 pm, on the 29th December 1870 in the canal, near the common bridge at Wisbeach, James W.Hooton of Wisbeach, threw himself flat on the ice, which broke and let him in, but he brought out a boy (8) and a girl (11).

Hugill, Henry J.   Medal   18813

At 6.15 pm, on the 15th August 1871, whilst at sea, Lieutenant A.H.Byng, R.N., Joseph Crabb, gunner's mate, and Henry Hugill, AB, jumped overboard from HMS *Resistance*, and saved John Long, captain of the main-top, same ship.

Bronze Medals to Lieutenant Byng and Joseph Crabb.

            Clasp   19319

At 11.20 am, on the 25th March 1873, at sea in the Firth of Clyde, Henry J.Hugill, AB, HMS *Black Prince*, jumped overboard, depth 50 fathoms, and supported Thomas Dummett, ordinary seaman, until a boat arrived.

Humphries, Charles Medal 22868-69

Charles Humphries, police constable, at great personal risk, rescued John Kerr from drowning, on the 10th August 1885, and rescued H.C.T.Jones from drowning, on the 15th August 1885. Both rescues were in the Floating Harbour, Bristol.

Clasp 23931

Charles Humphries, police constable, at great personal risk, rescued Richard Harvey from drowning at Bristol, on the 2nd May 1888.

Hunt, Hubert H. Medal 39174

At 1 am, on the 28th June 1912, a man fell from the sea gates at the East Basin, Cardiff Docks. Hubert H.Hunt, PC, and S.W.Wesgate went in and were successful in saving him.

Testimonial on parchment to Wesgate.

Clasp 40587

At 5.45 pm, on the 4th January 1914, a man named Mattey fell into the Roath Dock, Cardiff, in a dangerous position between a vessel and the quay. Thomas W.Harvey and Hubert H.Hunt, PC, went in and between them succeeded in saving the man.

Testimonial on vellum to Harvey.

Huntingford, W. Medal 30189

On the 8th August 1899, a woman fell from the pier at Clacton, the depth being 12 feet, with a strong ebb tide, there also being the danger of being carried under the SS *London Belle*. W.Huntingford, a seaman on board the vessel, at once sprang in, and with considerable difficulty and risk succeeded in saving the woman.

Clasp 33320

On the 28th June 1904, G.W.Abbott fell overboard from the steamer *Southend Belle* when nearing the landing stage at Margate. At great risk, W.Huntingford, 2nd mate, jumped in and supported him till they were picked up.

Hurcum, Charles Medal 34427

At 10.30 pm, on the 10th November 1905, a seaman in attempting to get on board HMS *Hecla*, fell into the sea at Kowloon, China. At great risk, Charles Hurcum, AB, plunged in from the ship and was successful in saving him.

Clasp 34539

At 6.30 am, on the 6th March 1906, W.C.Hopper accidentally fell overboard from a steamboat in Mirs Bay, China. At great risk, Charles Hurcum, leading seaman HMS *Hecla*, jumped after him and supported him for some time, but eventually had to let go and Hopper was drowned.

Isaacs, Harry J. Medal 23091

Harry J.Isaacs, clerk, at great personal risk, rescued William H.Godsell from drowning in the River Thames, at Reading, on the 22nd May 1886.

Clasp 25635

Harry J.Isaacs and George R.Ceily, at great personal risk, rescued a gentleman from drowning at Great Yarmouth, on the 30th August 1891.

Bronze Clasp to Ceily.

Jappy, James   Medal and Two Clasps   41455

On the nights of March 9th, 11th and 12th 1915, three men, owing to the absence of lights, fell into the harbour at Falmouth, the depth being 20 feet. On each occasion James Jappy, of the drifter *Thrive*, plunged in and effected the rescue.

Jermyn, John   Medal   21344

Lieutenant Jerram, RN, and Quartermaster J. Jermyn, HMS *Seaflower*, at great personal risk, rescued G. Butland, captain of the maintop, from drowning off St. Alban's Head, on the 12th July 1881. Dr. Pearson attended.

Bronze Medal to Lieutenant Jerram.

Clasp   22309

Thomas William Bell, quartermaster, HMS *Curaçoa*, and John Jermyn, ship's corporal same ship, at great personal risk, rescued Private Ogden, RMLI, from drowning in the River Woosing, China, on the 12th April 1884.

Silver Medal to Bell.

Clasp   24386

John Jermyn, ship's corporal, HMS *Lion*, at great personal risk, rescued Thomas W. Atkins from drowning, at Devonport, on 29th May 1889.

Johns, John   Medal   23765

John Johns, sailor, at great personal risk, rescued Philip Cloke from drowning at Mevagissey, Cornwall, on the 22nd September 1887.

Clasp   29042

John Johns, retired mariner, at great personal risk, rescued two boys from drowning in the harbour at Mevagissey, Cornwall, on the 19th August 1897.

Jubb, Benjamin B.   Medal   40583

On the night of the 12th December 1913, a seaman while returning to his ship fell into the dock at Portland, Oregon, USA. B.B.Jubb, apprentice on the barque *Hinemoa*, of Glasgow, left his bunk and plunging in held him till a rope was got and he was pulled out.

Clasp   42940

At 10.30 am, on the 14th August 1916, an insane man jumped overboard from his vessel at sea. Benjamin B.Jubb, 4th Officer of the ship, went after him and caught him, but when picked up nearly half an hour later the man did not recover.

Jutelet, J.G.   Medal   16350

On the 11th July 1859, J.Little of Dover, accidentally fell into the water in Dover Harbour. Captain J.G.Jutelet, of a French Mail Steamer, jumped in with his uniform on, and swam to his assistance and rescued him.

Clasp   19143

At 1.30 pm, on the 2nd June 1873, J.E.Simms, clerk of Walthamstow, fell into Calais Harbour, depth 12 feet. Captain Jutelet jumped overboard and saved the man.

Kemsley, H.H. Medal 41883

At 9.15 pm, on the 19th January 1915, a seaman accidentally fell overboard from his ship in Suva Harbour, Fiji, there being great danger from sharks. Acting Commander W.Burrows, R.N., and H.H.Kemsley, stewards officer, jumped in and kept him afloat till a boat reached them.

Bronze Medal to Commander Burrows.

Clasp 41884

At 6.20 pm, on the 26th February 1915, a seaman was in a boat which filled and sank in Suva Harbour, Fiji, the sea being choppy and great danger from sharks. H.H.Kemsley, stewards officer, and J.H.Cotton, stoker, went in and supported him till a boat reached them.

Bronze Medal to Cotton.

Lamport, Frederick W. Medal 19867

At 1.30 pm, on the 4th May 1876, at sea off Spithead, Frederick W.Lamport, AB, HMS *Excellent*, jumped overboard from the gun-boat *Skylark* into eight fathoms, to rescue A.McQuire, AB. The ship was steaming at six knots and he swam to the man and supported him until picked up.

Clasp 42616

At 9.10 pm, on the 2nd August 1916, a boy accidentally fell into the Thames at Lambeth in a dangerous position between a barge and the quay. Frederick Lamport, 1st class petty officer, Anti-Aircraft Corps, aged 64, jumped in but failed to find him.

Langdale, Frederick Lenox Medal 19399

At 2 pm, on the 7th March 1874, whilst at sea off Lisbon, Sub Lieutenant F.L.Langdale and Sub Lieutenant F.G.Langdon, of HMS *Resistance*, both jumped overboard into water 45 fathoms deep and tried to save Leading Seaman James Moore, who sank before being reached.

Bronze Medal also to Sub-Lieutenant F.G.Langdon.

Clasp 20089

At 5.15 pm, on the 16th January 1877, T.Martin, AB, HMS *Sapphire*, fell into the sea at Auckland, New Zealand. J.Lancaster, ordinary seaman and Sub Lieutenant F.L.Langdale, same ship, both jumped overboard, dived, and saved the man.

Bronze Medal to Lancaster.

Langdon, Frederick Gilbert Charles Medal 19399

At 2 pm, on the 7th March 1874, whilst at sea off Lisbon, Sub Lieutenant F.L.Langdale and Sub Lieutenant F.G.Langdon, both of HMS *Resistance*, both jumped overboard into water 45 fathoms deep and tried to save Leading Seaman James Moore, who sank before being reached.

Bronze Medal also to Sub-Lieutenant F.L.Langdale.

Clasp 30976

At 5 am, on the 23rd August 1900, a boy named Walmsley fell overboard from the Training Ship *Clio* at Bangor, North Wales into a strong tide. Commander F.G.C.Langdon was roused from bed, and going on deck, at once jumped after him, and held him up till they were taken on board a small boat.

Langton, George   Medal   21334-35

G.Langton, AB, HMS *Monarch*, on 20th June 1879, at great personal risk, rescued W. Stead, AB, from drowning in Phalerum Bay, and again, on the 29th December 1879, rescued E. Hunt, AB, who fell overboard in Malta Harbour.

Clasp   22214

George Langton, AB, of HMS *Stork*, at great personal risk, rescued W.T. Miller, OS, same ship, from drowning at Little Popo, West Coast of Africa, on the 23rd September 1883.

Lawrey, George   Medal   26905

George Lawrey, seaman, saved a man from drowning at Grace Harbour, Newfoundland, on the 22nd November 1893.

Clasp   26906

George Lawrey, salvor in the preceding case, saved a man from drowning at Grace Harbour on the 29th November 1893.

Leonard, Peter   Medal   23716

Sergeant Peter Leonard, R.I.C, at great personal risk, rescued Richard Callanane from drowning at Blackrock, Galway, on the 17th August 1887.

Clasp   24142

Sergeant Peter Leonard, R.I.C., Private John Bradley, Connaught Rangers, William Grieves and John Burns, at great personal risk, rescued Alexander Bain from drowning at Salthill, Galway, on the 25th August 1888.

Bronze Medals to Bradley, Grieves and Burns.

Lipscombe, Alfred   Medal   20440

At 1.30 pm, on the 6th August 1878, T.Bright of Newbury fell into the Kent and Avon Canal at Newbury, Berks. A.Lipscombe, publican, jumped into the water, swam to the spot, dived, caught the child, and brought it ashore.

Clasp   21791

Alfred Lipscombe, chairmaker, at great personal risk, rescued H.Jessett from drowning at Newbury, on the 12th August 1882.

Little, George   Medal   25714

George Little, labourer, at great personal risk, rescued Kate Westwood from drowning in the River Lee, at Bromley, on the 1st September 1891.

Clasp   26208

George Little, waterside labourer, at great personal risk, rescued John Harrington from drowning in the River Lee at Bromley, on the 29th September 1892. Pecuniary award also to Little.

Clasp   26900

George Little, labourer, at great personal risk, rescued Edward Reeve from drowning in the Lee Cut, at Bromley, on the 22nd November 1893.

Clasp   29460

On the 23rd June 1898. Alfred J.Clauson accidentally fell into Limehouse Cut, and was sinking under a barge. George Little, lighterman, at great risk, plunged in, and diving succeeded in bringing him to the bank.

Litton, James John　　　　　　　Medal　　　　　　　　　　　　　　20079

At 5.10 pm, on the 20th February 1877, C.H.Baker, boy 2nd class, fell overboard from HMS *Impregnable* into the sea at Devonport, the depth being 11 fathoms. James Litton, Acting Boatswain, same ship, jumped overboard and rescued the boy, who was unable to swim.

　　　　　　　　　　　　　　　　　　Clasp　　　　　　　　　　　　　　20347 -38

At 7.30 pm, on the 3rd May 1878, Matilda Coad and Alice Burnard fell into the canal at Devonport, nine feet deep and 30 feet from the shore. Mr J.J.Litton, boatswain, RN, HMS *Impregnable*, jumped into the water with all his clothes on, swam to the spot, and brought the children safe on shore.

Long, Frederick　　　　　　　　Medal　　　　　　　　　　　　　　21477

F.Long, AB, HMS *Alexandra*, at great personal risk, rescued L.Clench from drowning at sea, off Carthagena, on the 17th September 1881.

　　　　　　　　　　　　　　　　　　Clasp　　　　　　　　　　　　　　24078

Frederick Long, quartermaster, HMS *Excellent*, at great personal risk, rescued Stoker M.G.Didymus from drowning in Lough Swilly, on the 24th August 1888.

Lovering, Richard　　　　　　　Medal　　　　　　　　　　　　　　18090

At 7am, on the 23rd January 1868 at Ilfracombe Harbour, Richard Lovering, jumped, with all his clothes on, from the pier into 15 feet of water to rescue John New, a groom from Tors Park, Ilfracombe, and swam with him to the shore.

　　　　　　　　　　　　　　　　　　Clasp　　　　　　　　　　　　　　22617

Richard Lovering, boatman, at great personal risk, saved John Wills from drowning at Ilfracombe, on the 22nd December 1884.

Luccock, Thomas　　　　　　　 Medal　　　　　　　　　　　　　　15060

On the 10th June 1851, in the River Thames, Pool of London, T.Luccock, cook on board the *Gem*, jumped overboard and saved Henry Harris.

　　　　　　　　　　　　　　　　　　Clasp　　　　　　　　　　　　　　19236

At 6 pm, on the 8th September 1873, off West Pier, Scarborough, Thomas Luccock, mariner, jumped off the pier, depth eight feet, with sea boots on and brought out Martin Ingermill.

Mallon, Michael　　　　　　　　Medal　　　　　　　　　　　　　　26524

Michael Mallon, labourer, at great personal risk, rescued John Kenney from drowning in the Grand Canal at Edenderry, King's Co., on the 11th June 1893.

　　　　　　　　　　　　　　　　　　Clasp　　　　　　　　　　　　　　33745

On the 24th December 1904, Bridget Dempsey accidentally fell into the canal at Edenderry, King's Co., the canal being 18 yards wide and eight feet deep. Michael Mallon, at great risk, jumped in, and, having caught her, landed her on the opposite bank.

Martin, Robert W. Medal 30839

On the 20th April 1900, T.Conneely, stoker, HMS *Thetis*, fell from the ship into Durban Harbour. The depth was 21 feet, and the locality abounds with sharks. Robert W.Martin, petty officer, 2nd class, at great risk, sprang overboard, and was able to support him till a rope was got, and he was pulled on board.

Clasp 40632

At 2.10 pm, on the 3rd February 1914, the cutter *Snipe* while being towed by HMS *Leda* filled and sank in 40 feet of water three and a half miles off Clacton. Oswald C.Abbott, AB, who was on the cutter, was at once in difficulty and seeing this Robert W.Martin, gunner, who was also in the boat went to his help and supported him till they were picked up.

Martins, Robert Medal 19826

At 8.40am, on the 28th January 1876, at sea off Kingstown, Ireland, Robert Martins, yeoman of signals, jumped with all his clothes on, from the spar deck of HMS *Iron Duke*, a height of 24 feet, into the water. He caught boy 1st class David Levell by the collar and brought him to the surface, and supported him until the ship's boat arrived.

Clasp 20003

At 10am, on the 17th August 1876 at Kingstown, County Dublin, Robert Martins, yeoman of signals, jumped from the upper deck of HMS *Iron Duke*, into five fathoms of water and swam to E.N.Clark, AB, of the same ship. He succeeded in bringing Clark to the gangway, a distance of 30 yards, Clark having broken both arms in the fall.

Clasp 23341

Robert Martins, master-at-arms HMS *Royal Adelaide*, at great personal risk, rescued John W.Pearn from drowning at Devonport, on the 28th July 1886.

M(a)cAdam, Francis R.P. Medal 21355

Lieutenant McAdam, 1st Battalion, West Yorkshire Regiment, at great personal risk, rescued Lieutenant Lowry, and endeavoured to rescue a pilot, from drowning at Alderney, on the 23rd July 1881.

Clasp 25840

Captain F.R.P. MacAdam, 2nd Battalion, Yorkshire Regiment, at great personal risk, rescued Albert Wilson from drowning in the River Ouse, near York, on the 1st May 1892.

McAlister, William Medal 21803

W.McAlister, carpenter, at great personal risk, rescued a lady from drowning in the sea at Portrush, Co. Antrim, on the 6th September 1882. Dr Campbell attended.

Clasp 25049

William McAlister and Alfred Anderson, at great personal risk, rescued three ladies from drowning at Portrush, Co. Antrim, on the 16th August 1890.

Bronze Medal to Anderson.

McGhee, W. Medal 20933

At 2.45 pm, on the 30th May 1880, at Berehaven, W.McGhee, quartermaster, HMS *Minotaur*, jumped overboard, and with assistance rescued W.Davison, ordinary seaman.

Clasp 21497

W. McGhee, quartermaster, HMS *Warrior*, at great personal risk, rescued C.Allsop from drowning in the Clyde off Greenock, on the 22nd October 1881.

McLeod, Donald Medal 40548

At 11.50 pm, on the 29th November 1913, John Laird, an old man of 70, accidentally fell into the Queen's Dock, Glasgow, the night being dark and the depth 25 feet. Donald McLeod, police constable, plunged in and caught him, but when got into a boat he did not recover.

Clasp 42282

At 8.45 pm, on the 31st January 1916, a woman accidentally walked over the quay into the Clyde at Glasgow, the night being dark and the depth 26 feet. Donald McLeod, Police Constable, at once jumped in and caught her, and they were got out with a rope.

McLeod, Malcolm Medal 54007

At 1.30 am, on the 13th June 1937, Josephine G.Ogilvie (18) was sitting on the guard rails of Marine Parade when she fell into the sea, a depth of 12 feet. Sergeant Malcolm McLeod, Dover Constabulary, cycled to the spot, threw down a buoy rope and seeing that the girl was semi-conscious climbed down and supported her. It was impossible to land them so he was towed and swam with the girl 156 yards to the nearest landing stage. There was a heavy swell at the time.

Clasp 53306

At 12.30 pm, on the 3rd June 1939, six children between the ages of five and nine were having a picnic at the foot of the cliffs and were cut off by the rising tide. There was a strong S.E. wind and heavy seas at the time. Henry T.Blackett (29), who was bathing, swam to them and put them in a place of safety before wading and swimming back for help. Police Sergeant Malcolm McLeod, taking three lines, motored back to the cliff path, located the children below, and climbed down 330 feet caring for the children until a boat came. He then embarked them.

Bronze Medal to Blackett.

McVay, M. Medal 27836

Lance Corporal Corbett and Private M.McVay, 2nd Battalion, Northumberland Fusiliers, at great personal risk, attempted to rescue Private Colman, of the same regiment, who was unfortunately drowned at Fort Siloso, Singapore, on the 28th March 1895.

Clasp 28032

Privates M.McVay, M.Owen, J.Brown, and T.Miller, all of the 2nd Battalion, Northumberland Fusiliers, at great personal risk, rescued two men of the same regiment from drowning at Fort Siloso, Singapore, on the 11th April 1895.

Bronze Medals to Owen, Brown and Miller.

Moat, William Medal 19279

At 1 pm, on the 16th October 1873, at Whitby, William Moat jumped from the pier, a height of 20 feet into nine to ten feet of water and saved a child named William Austin.

Clasp 22057

William Moat, at great personal risk, rescued R. Swales from drowning at Whitby, Yorkshire, on the 3rd July 1883.

Monger, Harold G.R. Medal 46767

At 10.45 pm, on the 19th May 1923, E.J.Rapson fell overboard from a tug in Portland Harbour, a _ mile from shore, depth 28 feet, with the sea choppy and the night pitch dark. Harold G.R.Monger, water clerk, jumped from the tug and found him 30 yards away and took him back to the tug.

Clasp 47869

At 7.30 am, on the 7th July 1925, E.T.F.Phillips, deckhand, fell from a Coal Hulk, in a fit into 30 feet of water in Portland Harbour. Harold G.R.Monger, shipping clerk, went in from a tug by the hulk and, in spite of Phillip's strength, held him up till a boat reached them.

Montgomery, Donald Medal 18746

At 1 pm, on the 8th April 1871, at Pentland Skerries, Pentland Firth, George Alexander, ordinary seaman from Wick, fell into the water, six fathoms deep. Donald Montgomery, lighthouse keeper, swam through the surf and strong tide, and brought the man ashore.

Clasp 20041

At 11 am, on the 11th November 1876, offshore of Pollywilling, Southend, Argyll, New Brunswick, the barque *Faith of Irvine*, was in distress. Donald Montgomery, farmer, and Daniel Dempsey both went into the sea and assisted some of the crew to shore. They then went in a boat and rescued the remainder of the 13 man crew.

Vellum testimonial to Dempsey.

Moss, Josiah W. Medal 23484

Josiah W.Moss, fisherman, at great personal risk, rescued Michael Shea from drowning at Dingle, Ireland, on the 7th May 1887.

Clasp 25533

Joshua W.Moss, master of fishing boat, at great personal risk, rescued John Dunn from drowning at North Shields, on the 30th July 1891.

Neilson, Isaac Medal 35279

On the 4th May 1907, a boat with nine men on board was capsized on the Tyne at Hebburn, 30 yards from the side, in 15 to 20 feet of water. W.T.Martin, Isaac Neilson and D.R.Blaylock jumped in from the ferry steamer and supported all the men till they were picked up.

Bronze Medals also to Martin and Blaylock.

Clasp 36499

On the 24th December 1908, a man fell into the Tyne at Wallsend, the depth being 30 feet with a strong ebb tide and the night dark. F.H.Parkin and Isaac Neilson both went in, and between them succeeded in saving him.

Bronze Medal to Parkin.

Neno, John Medal 17345

On the 15th July 1864, at Plymouth harbour, John Neno, porter, plunged into the water, swam to the assistance of Edward Stowell, and rescued him.

| | Clasp | 18551 |

At 6.30 pm, on the 14th July 1870, at the North Corner, Devonport, John Neno plunged into 20 feet of water, with all his clothes on, and brought a girl named Susan Emmett to the quay.

Neville, Richard John Medal 22071

Richard Neville, aged 13, at great personal risk, rescued John Bennett from drowning at Folkestone, on the 24th July 1883.

| | Clasp | 22731 |

Richard John Nevill, fisher-boy, at great personal risk, saved William Baker from drowning in the harbour at Folkestone, on the 9th June 1885.

Newsham, John Medal 39335

At 2 pm, on the 6th August 1912, a man fell from the pier head into the channel at Barrow and became unconscious in 20 feet of water. John Newsham plunged in, swam 60 yards, and then supported him for 20 minutes, when a boat picked them up.

| | Clasp | 40229 |

At 10.45 pm, on the 5th August 1913, a man, in trying to land from a steamer, fell into the Walney Channel, Barrow, the depth being 28 feet. John Newsham plunged in to his help, but he was got out with a rope before Newsham reached him.

Newton, Hilary E. Medal 26863

Hilary E. Newton, gunner, at great personal risk, rescued Thomas Hammersley from drowning in the River Irrawaddy, Upper Burmah, on the 28th May 1893.

| | Clasp | 34773 |

On the 30th April 1906, a boy accidentally fell into the River Irrawaddy at Saging, there being a depth of 15 feet, with a strong current running. At great risk, Hilary E. Newton plunged in and succeeded in saving him.

Noble, Andrew Medal 22954

Andrew Noble, pilot, at great personal risk, rescued Charles Mundie from drowning at Fraserburgh, New Brunswick, on the 19th September 1885.

| | Clasp | 22955 |

Andrew Noble, pilot, at great personal risk, rescued George Strachan from drowning at Fraserburgh, New Brunswick, on the 28th October 1885.

Noel, Montague Wriothesley Medal 42270

At 6.25 pm, on the 3rd February 1916, a man accidentally fell overboard from HMS *Hindustan* in the Cromarty Firth, night very dark. Lieutenant M.W. Noel and Engineer Sub Lieutenant J.S. Erskine both jumped after him, but in the darkness failed to find him.

Bronze Medal to Erskine.

| | Clasp | 43853 |

At 9 pm, on the 8th October 1917, a man fell from his ship into the dock at Immingham, the depth being 20 feet, the night dark and raining. Lieutenant Montague W. Noel, R.N., went in fully clad and held him till he was got out with a rope.

North, Richard Medal 23543

Richard North, seaman, at great personal risk, rescued James Morris from drowning, at Corporation Pier, Hull, on the 10th June 1887.

Clasp 26309

Richard North, seaman, at great personal risk, rescued Alfred Welborn from drowning in the River Humber, at Hull, on the 16th December 1892.

Clasp 27751

Richard North, seaman, at great personal risk, rescued Charles Watson from drowning in the Humber, at Hull, on the 9th May 1895.

O'Connor, Patrick Medal 21276

P.O'Connor, at great personal risk, rescued G.Alford from drowning in the Thames, on the 12th May 1881

Clasp 22607

Patrick O'Connor, at great personal risk, rescued Charles Roberts from drowning in the River Thames, at Horselydown, on the 17th November 1884.

O'Sullivan, Charles Medal 21160

At 2 pm, on the 30th November 1880 at Ennis, C.O'Sullivan and A.S.Rice, Constables in the R.I.C., rushed into the River Fergus and rescued a lad named M.Hogan.

Testimonial on Parchment to Rice.

Clasp 22230

Charles O'Sullivan, Sergeant R.I.C., and John McMillan, constable, at great personal risk, rescued P.Guthrie from drowning at Ennis, Co. Clare, on the 27th January 1884.

Testimonial on vellum to McMillan.

Oakes, W.E. Medal 18935

At 6.45 pm, on the 7th July 1872, Samuel Collett fell into the River Thames at Westminster. W.E.Oakes, leaped off the steamboat *Citizen D* and succeeded in saving the man.

Clasp 19115

At 11.15 am, on the 12th April 1873, Mary Mills fell into the River Thames at London Bridge, depth 20 feet. W.E.Oakes, waterman, jumped overboard, swam to the woman, and helped to get her into a boat.

Clasp 19192

At 11.30 am, on the 13th July 1873, two men fell into the River Thames at Hammersmith, depth ten feet. W.E.Oakes, waterman, jumped overboard, fastened a rope round them, when they were drawn on board.

Oliver, William M. Medal and Clasp 18742

At 9.30 pm, on the 20th November 1870, Robert Jekyle fell into the River Darling. William M.Oliver, steward, jumped into the river with all his clothes on, and saved the man. At 10.30 pm on the 5th December 1870, Robert Grundry fell into the River Murray, South Australia. William M.Oliver, steward, again jumped into the river fully clothed and saved the man.

Panchen, Charles Medal 20221

At 8 am, on 21st August 1877 at Great Yarmouth, C.Panchen swam out from the South Beach into deep water and with difficulty brought Mr L.W.Stansell of Islington to the shore.

Clasp 22078

Charles Panchen, at great personal risk, rescued John Ellard from drowning at Great Yarmouth, on the 2nd July 1883.

Paton, Thomas Medal 18887

Harry Clist, private, jumped in and caught hold of Mrs Kemble and her child, and became entangled in her dress. Thomas Paton, veterinary surgeon, Army Service Corps, jumped in and helped to support them.

Clasp 19459

At 11.15 pm, on the 9th July 1874, at Portobello, Dublin, Thomas Paton, Army Service Corps, jumped into the Grand Canal, depth 8 to 10 feet, swam to John Ryan, medical student, and brought him to the bank and was assisted out.

Peebles, George Medal 22096

George Peebles, carpenter's crew, HMS *Cockatrice*, at great personal risk, rescued a gentleman from drowning in the River Danube, on the 5th July 1883.

Clasp 22097

George Peebles, William Sisley, AB and Henry J.Pratley, RMLI, HMS *Cockatrice*, at great personal risk, rescued a gentleman from drowning in the River Danube, on the 14th July 1883.

Bronze Medals to Sisley and Pratley.

Pengelly, Ernest Medal 42743

At 10.30 am, on the 30th July 1916, a woman carrying her child, in trying to board a steamer, fell into Mutton Cove, Plymouth. Ernest Pengelly, master mariner, jumped in and succeeded in saving both.

Clasp 43917

At 9 pm, on the 23rd November 1917, John Lucas (52) when leaving the steamer at Southdown, Plymouth, fell in and was carried under the paddle in 12 feet of water, the night being dark. Ernest Pengelly (36), Master Mariner of Plymouth, at once jumped in and going under the wheel got the man out and he was taken on board.

Petty, George Medal 18507

At 4 pm, on the 15th April 1870, Thomas Hamilton fell into the River Ouse at York, depth 15 feet. George Petty plunged into the water, swam 20 yards, and brought the man out.

Clasp 18565

At 2.30 pm, on the 25th June 1870, George Petty jumped into the water, swam to a boy named Thomas Anfield, and brought him out.

Phelps, Frederick Medal 17503

On 28th May 1865, Frederick Phelps, junior waterman of 3 Spring Gardens, Putney, swam to the relief of William and Mary Brown and child in the River Thames. They were then taken to the Swan Inn, Putney.

Pecuniary award to the landlord.

Clasp 23916

Frederick Phelps, waterman, at great personal risk, rescued Frederick P. Martin from drowning in the Thames at Putney, on the 27th March 1888.

Philpin, Richard Medal 24709

Richard Philpin, gunner, RA, at great personal risk, rescued Gunner O'Neill from drowning at Spithead, on the 2nd October 1889.

Clasp 29368

On the 25th March 1898, Richard Gaffney, gunner, RA, fell into the water between the SS *Falcon*, and the landing stage at Horse Sand Fort, Spithead. At the risk of being crushed between the steamer and the stage, Corporal Richard Philpin, 14th Co., S.D.R.A., jumped down and supported him till the vessel drifted clear and they were picked up.

Pigg, Joseph Medal 21914

Joseph Pigg, at great personal risk, rescued William Marshall from drowning in the River Eden, at Carlisle, on the 18th January 1883.

Clasp 22360

Joseph Pigg, joiner, at great personal risk, rescued George McVay from drowning in the River Eden, near Carlisle, on the 1st June 1884.

Pocklington, Archibald James Medal 19715

At 3 pm, on the 2nd September 1875, whilst at sea, lat.58° 5'N., long.1° 50'W., Henry Chandler, boy 1st class, fell overboard, depth 48 fathoms. Lieutenant A.J.Pocklington, R.N., HMS *Favourite*, jumped through the port quarter-port on the upper deck, seized the boy as he came to the surface, and supported him until picked up by the ship's cutter.

Clasp 20275

At 8.10 am, on the 20th September 1877, whilst at sea, W.D.Herbert, ordinary seaman, HMS *Rover*, fell into the sea. Lieutenant A.J.Pocklington, R.N., same ship, jumped from the poop, swam to the man, and with a life buoy supported him until assistance arrived; the spot abounded with sharks.

Poë, Edmund Samuel Medal 19632

At 4.07 am, on the 14th May 1875, in the Atlantic Ocean, lat. 10° 15'N., long. 21° 39'W., William Duncanson, AB, fell overboard. Lieutenant E.S.Poë jumped overboard from the hammock nettings, swam to the man, and supported him to a life buoy. Commander J.H.Dacres jumped out of his cabin port, swam to the man, and aided in supporting him to the life buoy.

Bronze Clasp to Comdr. Dacres.

Clasp 20047

At 11 am, on the 18th October 1876, at Woosung, China, Lewis Sampson, stoker, HMS *Immortalite* fell into the water. Lieutenant E.S.Poë, HMS *Newcastle*, jumped overboard, and supported the man until picked up by a boat.

Potter, James   Medal   18621

At 7.30 pm, on the 15th August 1870, at North Beach, Lowestoft, James Potter plunged into the sea, depth 15 feet, swam and brought Mr Lonsdale ashore.

           Clasp   19408

At 7.30 am, on the 14th July 1874 at Lowestoft, Suffolk, Sergeant James Potter, drill-instructor, 17th Suffolk Rifle Volunteers, swam out 70 yards and brought John Allsopp ashore.

Prescott, John   Medal   22335

John Prescott, AB, HMS *Swift*, at great personal risk, rescued John Moore, AB, from drowning at Amoy, China, on the 7th May 1884.

           Clasp   26865

John Prescott, petty officer, HMS *St.Vincent*, at great personal risk, rescued H.Critchell from drowning at Portsmouth, on the 10th October 1893.

Prinsep, J.F.M.   Medal   22686

Lieutenant J.F.M.Prinsep, 2nd Battalion, Essex Regiment, at great personal risk, saved George Wheeler from drowning in the River Nile, at the Shaban Rapid, on the 23rd December 1884.

           Clasp   23020

Lieutenant J.F.M.Prinsep, the Essex Regiment, at great personal risk, rescued a Soudanese sailor from drowning in the River Nile, near El Sabon, on the 19th December 1885.

Pritchard, Robert   Medal   18320

At 8.10 am, on the 3rd June 1869 at the Old Harbour, Holyhead, Robert Pritchard jumped into the sea, depth 22 feet, with heavy working clothes on, and brought a boy, Robert Jones, to the surface and saved him.

           Clasp   19407

At 2.30 pm, on the 4th July 1874, at the landing stage at Holyhead, Robert Pritchard, coastguard, jumped into seven fathoms of water, dived, and brought a child named F.P.Bunting to the surface, and swam with him to shore.

Puttock, Robert   Medal   23391

Robert Puttock, leading seaman, HMS *Audacious*, at great personal risk, rescued John Haley, boy 1st class, from drowning at Hakodate Harbour, Japan, on the 27th September 1887.

           Clasp   23906

Lieutenant Charles W.P.Allen, R.N. and Robert Puttock, captain of the mast, HMS *Audacious*, at great personal risk, rescued Jack T.Poole, AB, from drowning at Hong Kong, on the 7th February 1888.

Bronze Medal to Lieutenant Allen.

Quigley, Patrick   Medal   18276

At 10.30 pm, on the 19th December 1868, James Breen fell from the Quay at New Ross in Ireland into 20 feet of water. Patrick Quigley, sailor, ran about 300 yards, jumped into the water with clothes on, and saved the man.

                                    Clasp   18855

At 8 pm, on the 2nd September, Thomas Butler fell into the water at Corfu. Patrick Quigley, seaman on the Yacht *Mari uita*, jumped into the water and saved him. On 18th December 1871 at 1 am, when at Naples, a man fell into four fathoms of water. Quigley again jumped in and saved the man.

Quince, J.   Medal   20215

At 8 am, on the 26th August 1877, off the South Beach, Great Yarmouth, a man was in difficulty in 20 feet of water. J. Quince, Sergeant-Major, Norfolk Artillery Militia, went into the sea, swam to the man, and with difficulty brought him to shore.

                                    Clasp   21703

Sergeant Major J.Quinn, R.A., at great personal risk, rescued R.Symonds from drowning at Great Yarmouth on the 12th July 1882. (Name changed from Quince to Quinn).

Renforth, Stephen   Medal   25070

Stephen Renforth, waterman, at great personal risk, rescued William Baker from drowning in the River Tyne, at Gateshead, on the 5th August 1890.

                                    Clasp   27537

Stephen Renforth, at great personal risk, rescued P.Burke from drowning in the Tyne, at Gateshead, on the 26th January 1895.

                                    Clasp   30122

On the 13th June 1899, a child fell into the Tyne at Newcastle, the depth at the time being 12 feet. Stephen Renforth, who was in bad health at the time, plunged in from the quay and, at great risk, supported it until a boat came. When the boat came it was pulled right over Renforth, cutting his head open, and he was taken from the water in an exhausted state.

Rix, James   Medal   18728

At 1 pm, on 16th May 1871 at Richmond, Surrey, James Rix ran to the bank of the River Thames and plunged in with his clothes on. He brought out a child named William Callacott.

                                    Clasp   22022

James Rix, at great personal risk, rescued Sybil Messum from drowning in the River Thames, at Richmond, on the 19th June 1883.

Robe, John   Medal   19164

At 3.30pm, on the 22nd June 1873 at South Shields, John Robe, an iron shipwright, plunged into the River Tyne at a depth of 8 feet, and brought out a child named E.Webster.

                                    Clasp   22770

John Robe, boilermaker, at great personal risk, saved two boys from drowning in the Albert Edward Dock, North Shields, on the 9th July 1885.

Roberts, Ben Medal 20398

At 11.30 am, on the 31st May 1878, at Cape Point, Cape of Good Hope, a boat capsized 60 yards from shore, with breakers 14 feet high. J.Andrews, King George and Ben Roberts, kroomen, HMS *Flora*, rushed into the sea to the rescue of the three men, A.Gilham, R.Gray, carpenters and Staff Commander J.C.Tolflect, R.N. They were in great danger of drowning by the capsizing of the whaleboat, and with great difficulty the kroomen succeeded in saving two lives.

Bronze Medals to J.Andrews and King George.

Clasp 20822

On 19th August 1879 at Sierra Leone, G.L.Creed, leading seaman fell into the water. B.Roberts, AB, P.Brown, AB, and G.Bridge, ordinary seaman, HMS *Dido*, all jumped overboard to the rescue of the man, swam with him, and succeeded in bringing him to the gangway.

Bronze Medals to Brown and Bridge.

Robertson, R. Medal 36202

On the 13th August 1908, John McKie accidentally fell into the dock at Ayr, there being a depth of 14 feet. Lance Corporal R.Robertson, Royal Scots Fusiliers, jumped in and was successful in saving him.

Clasp 36904

On the 12th August 1909, David Turner fell into the river at Ayr, there being a depth of 16 feet. Lance Corporal R.Robertson, Royal Scots Fusiliers, plunged in from the quay and rescued him.

Ross, A.D. Medal 14703

On the 29th December 1868, Mr A.D.Ross, deputy dock master, plunged into the Regent's Canal Dock and rescued a boy.

Clasp 19182

At 2.30 pm, on the 5th July 1873, A.D.Ross, pilot, jumped into the River Thames at Gravesend, depth seven feet, and brought out a boy named J.Row.

Rowland, Alexander Medal 26197

Constable Alexander Rowland, E Division, Metropolitan Police, at great personal risk, attempted to rescue William F.Skinner from drowning in the Thames at Wandsworth, on the 15th September 1892.

Clasp 27052

Alexander Rowland, at great personal risk, attempted to rescue a man, name unknown, from drowning in the Thames at Charing Cross, 23rd May 1894.

Sailing, Laurence (Lawrence) Medal 33277

On the 23rd June 1904, Harry Randle, while bathing in the Lea, was seized with cramp in 10 feet of water. Laurence Sailing, who has a wooden leg, went in, and, at great risk, rescued him.

Clasp 39964

At 2 pm, on the 3rd June 1913, a youth named Carter was bathing in a lake at Edmonton, the depth being over 10 feet, and got into difficulty. Lawrence Sailing, who has only one leg, went in, and after diving many times found him and got him out, but he did not recover. Pecuniary award also to Sailing.

Sandilands, Hon. Francis Robert　　　Medal　　　　　　　　　　　　　　　19593

At 1 am, on the 1st January 1875 whilst at sea (lat. 15° 44'N, long. 58°29'E), Lieutenant Hon. F.R. Sandilands, R.N., jumped overboard from HMS *Audacious*, and swam to ship's corporal F.Cowd who had fallen overboard. He supported him for a quarter of an hour until a boat arrived.

　　　　　　　　　　　　　　　　　　　Clasp　　　　　　　　　　　　　　　22602

Commander the Hon. F.R.Sandilands, R.N., HMS *Asia*, at great personal risk, rescued N.Smith (AB) from drowning in Portsmouth Harbour, on the 19th November 1884.

Sayce, Henry　　　　　　　　　　　　Medal　　　　　　　　　　　　　　　35280

On the 3rd May 1907, A.P.Truscott, an AB, threw himself from a boat into Portsmouth harbour. Henry Sayce, Petty Officer, HMS *Excellent*, jumped in and rescued him in an unconscious state.

　　　　　　　　　　　　　　　　　　　Clasp　　　　　　　　　　　　　　　44619

At 10.20 pm, on the 26th November 1918, T.H.Rowlands fell into the River Mersey near the Princes Stage, Liverpool, the night was dark and there was a strong ebb tide. Henry Sayce, Customs Watcher, Liverpool, jumped in and got Rowlands into a lifebuoy, and he was then taken into a boat.

Sayer, Henry　　　　　　　　　　　　Medal　　　　　　　　　　　　　　　25850

Henry Sayer, at great personal risk, rescued Arthur Franklin from drowning in the Regent's Canal at Shoreditch, on the 25th April 1892.

　　　　　　　　　　　　　　　　　　Clasp　　　　　　　　　　　　　　　25894

Henry Sayer, at great personal risk, rescued Albert G. Holmes from drowning in the Regent's Canal, at Hackney, on the 7th June 1892.

　　　　　　　　　　　　　　　　　　　Clasp　　　　　　　　　　　　　　　26463

Henry Sayer, timber porter, at great personal risk, rescued E. Pickersgill from drowning in the Regent's Canal, at Haggerston, on the 15th May 1893.

　　　　　　　　　　　　　　　　　　　Clasp　　　　　　　　　　　　　　　26603

Henry Sayer, labourer, at great personal risk, rescued William Firm from drowning in the Regent's Canal, at Haggerston, on the 27th June 1893.

　　　　　　　　　　　　　　　　　　　Clasp　　　　　　　　　　　　　　27727-28

Henry Sayer, a deal porter, at personal risk, rescued two boys from drowning in the Regent's Canal, on the 4th and 19th May 1895.

　　　　　　　　　　　　　　　　　　　Clasp　　　　　　　　　　　　　　　36880

On the 10th August 1909, a boy fell into the Regent's Canal at Hackney and sank in 10 feet of water. Henry Sayer jumped in from a height of 14 feet, and, after diving, succeeded in saving him.

Scaife, Henry Neale Medal 14988

On 20th May 1850, in Portsmouth harbour, Mr H.Neale Scaife, clerk of HM Yacht *Victoria and Albert*, rushed on deck, and jumped overboard and saved a marine.

Clasp 19097

At 11 pm, on the 3rd February 1873, at the New Mole, Gibraltar, H.N.Scaife, paymaster, R.N., and Edward Aldridge, able seaman, both jumped overboard and brought John De Vries, paymaster, R.N., to the shore, the depth being 20 feet and the night very dark.

Setter, Frederick W. Medal 41382

At 9.54 am, on the 14th February 1915, a boat with eight men on board was capsized alongside one of HM ships at sea. F.W.Setter, PO, F.G.Selwood, PO, A.N.Bennett, Leading Signalman, George Ward, AB, W.R.Cape, AB, S.McD.Ballantyne, AB and Eugene Murphy, PO, all jumped in from the ship and exerted themselves in saving or attempting to save life. Eugene Murphy unfortunately lost his own life after saving one man.

Bronze Medal to each, 'In Memorium' to relatives of Murphy.

Clasp 45457

At 6.20 pm, on the 17th June 1920, Edgar Flynn (9) fell overboard from a motor launch in Invergordon Harbour about 50 yards from the pontoon. The water was 18 feet deep and there was a two knot tide. Percy Ripley (20), AB, went in and caught him but got into difficulties. Frederick W.Setter (31), Petty Officer, then went in and rescued both.

Unsuccessful vellum to Ripley.

Setter, James H. Medal 35741

On the 27th October 1907, a boy fell from a landing stage into the Thames at Southwark, the depth being 12 feet with a strong tide. James H.Setter, constable, Metropolitan Police, jumped in and rescued him.

Clasp 39615

At 5.40 pm, on the 13th October 1912, a woman threw herself into the Thames from the Albert Embankment. Paul Tarditi went in but failed to reach her and was picked up by boat. Sergeant J.H.Setter, Metropolitan Police, then swam out and got her to the side, but she did not recover.

Pecuniary award to Tarditi.

Shapter, Joseph Medal 20082

At 4 pm, on the 1st February 1877, at Rock Ferry, Joseph Shapter, AB, HMS *Achilles*, jumped overboard and supported C.J.Crocker, ordinary seaman, same ship, until a boat arrived.

Clasp 21729

J.Shapter, captain's coxswain HMS *Algerine*, at great personal risk, rescued several persons from a capsized boat on the West Coast of Africa on the 30th March 1882.

Shooter, Frank   Medal   19165

At 6.30 pm, on the 5th June 1873, at the Weir Head, Exeter, Devon, Frank Shooter, jumped into the river, depth 10 feet, and with considerable difficulty and risk, brought F.Prothero to land.

                                       Clasp   19503

At 7.30 am, on the 7th August 1874, Frank Shooter, bathing attendant, jumped into the River Exe at Exeter, with all his clothes on, swam to a lad named E.H.Gibson, and brought him to the bank.

                                       Clasp   20230

At 5.30 pm, on the 31st July 1877, F.Shooter plunged into the River Exe at Exeter, depth 15 feet, and with difficulty rescued Private W.Knott, 11th Regiment.

                                       Clasp   22058

Frank Shooter, at great personal risk, rescued H.Standlake from drowning at Exeter, on the 4th June 1883.

                                       Clasp   22472

Frank Shooter, at great personal risk, rescued Frank Nicks from drowning at Exeter, on the 7th July 1884.

Slaughter, Frank   Medal   25602

Frank Slaughter, waterman, at great personal risk, rescued Charles Morris from drowning at Littlehampton, on the 8th September 1891.

                                       Clasp   27711

Frank Slaughter, innkeeper, at great personal risk, rescued D.H.Moore from drowning at Arundel, on the 2nd June 1895.

                                       Clasp   30829

On the 15th August 1900, a girl named Clarke fell into 8 to 10 feet of water in the Arun at Bury, Sussex. At great risk, Frank Slaughter, waterman, jumped in and rescued her.

Smith, Charles Henry   Medal   22274

Charles H.Smith, seaman, at great personal risk, rescued Private Griffin, York and Lancaster Regiment, from drowning at Dover, on the 23rd April 1884.

                                       Clasp   22703

Charles H.Smith, senior mate in command of HM Cruiser *Spy*, at great personal risk, saved C.Cheeseman from drowning at Portsea, on the 16th May 1885.

                                       Clasp   23373

Charles Henry Smith, waterman, at great personal risk, rescued Bombardier Thomas Birtwhistle, R.M.A., from drowning at Portsea, on the 12th December 1886.

Smith, Henry G.   Medal   21962

Henry Smith, at great personal risk, rescued J.Arthur from drowning in the Harbour, Newhaven, on the 31st March 1883.

                                 Clasp   23361

Henry Andrews, Henry G.Smith, John Upton and John Hulse, all of HMS *Briton*, rescued Charles Rosevear, same ship, from drowning in Bombay Harbour, on the 29th September 1886.

Bronze Medal to Andrews; Vellums to Upton and Hulse.

Smith, Richard   Medal   18801

Richard Smith, swam out between two and three hundred yards to a boy named Alexander Townsend, and brought him ashore.

                                 Clasp   25954

Richard Smith, dock labourer, at great personal risk, rescued Walter Barnes from drowning in Millwall Dock, on the 23rd May 1892.

Spinner, Charles   Medal   20592

At 5 pm, on the 28th May 1879, C.Spinner, AB, HMS *Raleigh*, whilst at sea, jumped overboard, and with great difficulty attempted to rescue D.Cook, leading seaman, but without success.

                                 Clasp   29256

Charles Spinner, at great personal risk, rescued B.Morris from drowning in the sea at Dover, on the 5th November 1897.

Stark, Frederick   Medal   33630

On the 25th September 1904, G.Livesay fell from the quay into the harbour at Leith, the depth being 15 feet with a strong tide. Frederick Stark, boatman, at great risk, jumped in from a height of 18 feet, and, having caught the boy, they were both got out with a lifebuoy.

                                 Clasp   35846

On the 24th December 1907, a boy accidentally fell into the harbour at Leith, the depth being 16 feet, and the water very foul. Frederick Stark jumped in from a height of 20 feet and with difficulty succeeded in saving him.

Startin, James   Medal   19895

At 1.45 pm, on the 27th May 1876 at Bashika Bay, Midshipman Mr.J.Startin of HMS *Invincible*, jumped overboard and caught Ordinary Seaman David Forbes, placed him on his back, and remained with him until rescued by the cutter.

                                 Clasp   22095

Lieutenant James Startin, RN, and Assistant Paymaster Denham R.Kelsey, HMS *Cockatrice*, at great personal risk, rescued J.Pappadoles from drowning in the River Danube on the 10th June 1883.

Bronze Medal to Kelsey.

                                 Clasp   32509

On the 9th March 1903, a seaman fell overboard from HMS *Arethusa*, off Sheerness. Captain J. Startin, at great risk, jumped from the ship and supported him till they were picked up by a boat.

Streader, William T. Medal 17271

On 11th January 1864, Austen Baxter fell through the ice on the canal at Wisbeach. William T.Streader went on a ladder on the ice to his relief, became immersed, but eventually rescued him.

Clasp 19560

At 10 am, on the 16th December 1874, Robert Brazier, pilot, was in danger in the sea at Shoreham, Sussex. W.T.Streader swam through the heavy surf with a life line and succeeded in bringing the man to the beach, but he could not be revived.

Sullivan, Timothy John Medal 25349

Timothy J.Sullivan, AB, HMS *Cleopatra*, at great personal risk, rescued John Leaman from drowning off Monte Video, on the 4th April 1891.

Clasp 25743

Timothy J.Sullivan, AB, HMS *Cleopatra*, at great personal risk, rescued Private J.H.King, R.M.L.I., from drowning at Ensenada, Monte Video, on the 13th November 1891.

Clasp 25897

Timothy J.Sullivan, AB, HMS *Cleopatra*, at great personal risk, rescued B.M.Mitchell, from drowning at Monte Video, on the 21st January 1892.

Swan, Stewart F. Medal 39790

At 7 pm, on the 4th February 1913, a woman accidentally fell from the quay into the harbour at Cork, there being a depth of 16 feet. Stewart F.Swan, chief officer of the SS *Kenmare*, plunged in and caught her, and they were lifted out by a crane chain.

Clasp 41537

At 10.45 pm, on the 11th May 1915, a man fell overboard from a steamer in the harbour at Fishguard, the depth being 30 feet and the night dark. Stewart F.Swan jumped in and held him till a boat reached them.

Taylor, Joseph G. Medal 36809

On the 4th July 1909, a boy fell into the Thames at Chelsea, the depth being 12 feet with a strong cross-current running. Joseph G.Taylor, constable, Metropolitan Police, plunged in and was able to swim with him to a disused pier, to which he held till a boat picked them up.

Clasp 39279

At 4.30 pm, on the 20th July 1912, a boy fell into the Thames at Chelsea, the depth being 12 feet with a strong current running. Joseph Taylor, constable, Metropolitan Police, plunged in but failed to effect the rescue, the boy being drowned.

Touhey, Willliam Medal 43399

On the 28th May 1917, a man in an attempt at suicide jumped overboard from his ship at Solombala, there being a strong current running. William Touhey, Seaman, at once went after him and kept him afloat till a boat picked them up.

Clasp 43526

On the 31st May 1917, a Russian boy fell into Solombala Harbour and was being carried away, the depth being 15 feet and very cold. William Touhey, Seaman, SS *Bontnewydd*, plunged in and succeeded in bringing him out.

Trafford, William Leigh　　　　　Medal　　　　　　　　　　　　27528

William Leigh Trafford, assisted by Miss M.L.Trafford, at great personal risk, rescued Edwin Harrison from drowning in the River Ouse at Biddenham, on the 9th February 1895. Vellum to Miss Trafford.

　　　　　　　　　　　　　　　　　Clasp　　　　　　　　　　　　29006

W.Trafford, City of Edinburgh Volunteer Artillery, at great personal risk, gallantly attempted to rescue W.Hamilton, who was unfortunately drowned while bathing at Shoeburyness, on the 4th August 1897.

Tremayne, George　　　　　　Medal　　　　　　　　　　　　35140

On the 2nd February 1907, a boy named Bethel accidentally fell overboard from the Training-ship *Clio* at Bangor, North Wales. There was a two-knot tide and the weather very cold. George Tremayne, chief officer, jumped in from a boat, and diving, caught the boy and succeeded in saving him.

　　　　　　　　　　　　　　　　　Clasp　　　　　　　　　　　　37318

On the 9th April 1910, a boy fell overboard from the Training-ship *Clio* in the Menai Straits at Bangor, the tide being strong and the weather cold. George Tremayne, chief officer, at once jumped after him and kept him afloat till they were picked up by a boat.

Turner, Henry C.　　　　　　　Medal　　　　　　　　　　　　23652

Henry, C.Turner, captain of quarter-deck men, R.N., at great personal risk, rescued two women from drowning, at Spithead, on the 24th July 1887.

　　　　　　　　　　　　　　　　　Clasp　　　　　　　　　　　　24794

Henry C.Turner, petty officer, HMS *Invincible*, at great personal risk, rescued Gunner John Younger from drowning off Netley, on the 13th March 1890.

Vaughan, John Owen　　　　　Medal　　　　　　　　　　　　23204

John Owen Vaughan, bathing attendant, at great personal risk, rescued Mary W.Dod from drowning at Rhyl, on the 6th August 1886.

　　　　　　　　　　　　　　　　　Clasp　　　　　　　　　　　　23668

John Owen Vaughan, bathing machine proprietor, at great personal risk, rescued three persons from drowning at Rhyl, North Wales, on the 1st August 1887.

Vaughan-Jones, Hubert　　　　Medal　　　　　　　　　　　　33489

On the 15th August 1904, a man named Hurst fell from a barge which was fast astern of HMS *Exmouth* in Portland Roads. Acting Sub-Lieutenant H.Vaughan-Jones jumped in, at great risk, but failed to find him, and Hurst was drowned.

　　　　　　　　　　　　　　　　　Clasp　　　　　　　　　　　　37048

On the 15th July 1909, Lieutenant F.F.Ormonde fell overboard from submarine *C* off the Shipwash Light. Lieutenant H.Vaughan-Jones and R.O.Atkinson, AB, jumped in and supported him till they were picked up by a boat.

Bronze Medal to Atkinson.

Vingoe, Alfred   Medal   22631

Alfred Vingoe, boy of Training-ship *Mount Edgecumbe*, at great personal risk, saved William Weeks, boy, same ship, from drowning at Saltash, on the 28th January 1885.

                                        Clasp   23660

Alfred Vingoe and Richard G.Harris, boys 1st class, HMS *Sealark*, at great personal risk, rescued Thomas Driscoll from drowning at Plymouth, on the 12th July 1887.

Bronze Medal to Harris.

Wackerell, George William   Medal   26068

George William Wackerell, AB, HMS *Northampton*, at great personal risk, rescued William H.England from drowning off Falmouth on the 29th July 1892.

                                        Clasp   28217

George W.Wackerell, petty officer 1st class, HMS *Tourmaline*, at great personal risk, rescued J.McSweeny, AB, from drowning at Port Royal, Jamaica, on the 5th February 1896.

Waters, Michael   Medal   23072

Michael Waters, master shipwright, at great personal risk, rescued Charles Hambley from drowning in the Floating Dock, Limerick, on the 27th March 1886.

                                        Clasp   24251

Michael Waters, foreman shipwright, at great personal risk, rescued two persons from drowning at Limerick, on the 20th December 1888.

                                        Clasp   25372

Michael Waters, master shipwright, at great personal risk, rescued Mr Dally from drowning at Limerick, on the 9th April 1891.

Watkins, Milson   Medal   26623

Milson Watkins, chimney sweep, at great personal risk, rescued Frederick L.Phillips from drowning in the River Wye, at Monmouth, on the 1st July 1893.

                                        Clasp   35791

On the 23rd December 1907, a boy fell into the Wye at Monmouth, the river being in flood, 12 to 14 feet deep, and very cold. Milson Watkins plunged in and was successful in saving the lad.

Watson, John Medal 27450

John Watson, at great personal risk, rescued A.Mackie from drowning at Invergordon, 28th November 1894.

Clasp 29787

On the 1st October 1898, a boy fell into the harbour at Leith, the depth being 12 feet. John Watson, shipwright, at great risk, plunged in, and after diving brought him to the surface, and they were then pulled on to the quay by a rope.

Clasp 41276

At 8.20 pm, on the 19th September 1914, two soldiers of the Black Watch accidentally fell into the harbour at Cromarty, the depth being 18 feet with a strong tide, and the night dark. John Watson, a ferryman, plunged in and succeeded in saving both men.

Clasp 41280

At 8 pm, on the 11th November 1914, a man accidentally fell from the pier into the harbour at Cromarty, and was carried out 30 yards, the sea being choppy with a strong tide. John Watson, ferryman, plunged in and with difficulty saved him.

Clasp 45187

At 7.15 pm, on the 13th September 1919, a man fell overboard from the ferry half a mile from the shore at Cromarty. There was a strong ebb tide going at eight knots. John Watson (54) at once went into the sea after the man and kept him up for 15 minutes when they were picked up.

Watts, Henry Medal 18244

At 7 am, on the 21st August 1868, a boy named John Fox fell into the River Wear, depth 12 feet. Henry Watts, diver, jumped into the river and brought him out. Watts was noted as having participated in former acts of lifesaving.

Clasp 25844

Henry Watts, diver, at great personal risk, rescued Alfred Fatherley from drowning in the dock at Sunderland, on the 8th May 1892.

Wenlock, Walter B. Medal 36234

On the 11th August 1908, a boat with two persons on board was capsized in 12 feet of water in the Hamble near Southampton. Walter Wenlock, captain of a yacht, jumped in from a boat and rescued the lady and also assisted in saving her companion.

Clasp 42411

At 6 am, on the 17th April 1916, a man fell overboard from his ship as she was leaving the harbour at Stornaway. Lieutenant W.B.Wenlock, R.N.R., jumped after him fully clothed and kept him afloat till they were got on board with a lifebuoy.

West, Daniel Medal 24782

Daniel West, fisherman, at great personal risk, rescued James Buick from drowning at Montrose, New Brunswick, on the 28th February 1890.

Clasp 53735

At 3.30 pm on the 3rd October 1936, at Montrose, George Cuthbert (5) was playing with a younger brother and fell into the river and sank 12 feet from the bank, there being a strong flood tide. Daniel West (81), ex pilot of Montrose, took off his heavy clothes and dived five feet into the water ten feet deep. He raised the boy from the bottom and swam 45 yards along the river, and getting the younger boy to lower a rope, hung on till help arrived. West was in the water for _ an hour.

Whyte, Charles   Medal   18347

At noon on the 4th July 1869, Charles Whyte swam out to a depth of 18 feet in a pond at Hampstead and brought James Allen back to the shore.

                                   Clasp   22635

Charles Whyte, swimming master, at great personal risk, saved a man, name unknown, from drowning in Highgate Pond, on the 25th January 1885.

Williams, James   Medal   18256

At 9 am, on the 13th August 1868, at Sydney, New South Wales, H.W.Glazbrook, 1st class boy, fell overboard from HMS *Blanche*, into nine fathoms of water. James Williams, boatswain, same ship, jumped overboard with all his clothes on from the top-gallant forecastle, and saved him.

                                   Clasp   18479

At 5.30 pm, on the 27th September 1869, HMS *Blanche* was at sea, lat. 57°S., long. 160°E., when Thomas Powell, boy 1st class, fell overboard. James Williams, boatswain, jumped overboard, with the ship going at seven knots, placed a life buoy over the boy's head, and held him until picked up.

Woods, Henry Byron   Medal   17979

On the 5th July 1867 at Pangbourne, Berkshire, Lieutenant H.B.Woods, R.M.L.I., threw himself from an outrigger into the River Thames, and swam to two persons and saved them.

                                   Clasp   23272

Captain Henry Byron Woods, R.M.L.I., at great personal risk, rescued three persons from drowning in the Thames, at Streatley, on the 11th July 1886.

Wray, George H.   Medal   18342

At noon, on the 5th May 1869, at sea near Rasmadraka, south east coast of Africa, two slave children and F.Trebilcock, ordinary seaman, HMS *Dryad*, were in difficulties. Jim George swam to shore with the two children. George H.Wray swam to shore with Trebilcock, and assisted in saving the others.

Bronze Medal to Jim George.

                                   Clasp   19185

At 1.30 pm, on the 28th May 1873, Joseph Tyson, gunner, R.M.A., fell overboard at lat. 15° 6', long.23° 24'. George H.Wray, ordinary seaman, HMS *Barracoutta*, jumped overboard and tried unsuccessfully to save him, the ship going at a speed of five to eight knots.

Wright, Walter John   Medal   22272

Walter J.Wright, at great personal risk, rescued Rosine Tait from drowning in the River Thames at Vauxhall Bridge, on the 10th March 1884.

                                   Clasp   23126

Walter John Wright, engine driver, at great personal risk, rescued Henry Tapling from drowning in the River Thames, at Horsleydown, on the 1st July 1886.

Young, Charles E.   Medal   27826

C.E.Young, at great personal risk, rescued W.Cope from drowning in the Thames at Woolwich, on the 18th July 1895.

Clasp   38179

At 1.40 pm, on the 7th June 1911, a lad while bathing in the Thames at Woolwich was carried out 20 yards and sank in deep water. Charles Young swam out and, diving, found him and brought him to land.

Young, Henry L.   Medal   18473

At 4.45 pm on the 23rd February 1870, Henry L.Young jumped into the canal at Shrewsbury with all his clothes on, swam to a boy named Henry B.Hodgson, and brought him out.

Clasp   18735

At 3.30 pm on the 24th May 1871, a student, Roland O'Regan, fell into the River Severn at Shreswbury, depth 12 feet. Henry L.Young, student, caught hold of O'Regan, supported him, and brought him to the shore in an insensible state.

INDICES

INDEX TO STANHOPE MEDALS

Aspeslet, Malcom Rodney	13	Ledden, Aaron John	26
Bailey, Vanessa	29	McNab, John	17
Beale, Ivor Laurence	5	McPherson, Bruce Walter	16
Broekmeulen, John Christopher	12	Moore, Lesley Allison	24
Broughton, Ian Maurice	27	Nicol, Thomas	12
Calnan, David	30	Novis, Rupert	22
Campbell, Barry John	9	O'Sullivan, Hugh Barry	6
Davey, Randy Sherman	15	Peters, Rodney Stephen	24
Day, Anthony Shane	28	Robertson, William	7
Easton, Jack Milne	11	Robson, Graham Thomas	14
Fader, Douglas	26	Ryan, Robert John	11
Garner, David Michael	20	Shemmedi, Mehmet Mustafa	5
Gill, Thomas F.	4	Smith, Beryl Ellen	25
Gleeson, Terry Haydon	14	Smith, James George	21
Golding, Victor Leonard	19	Sonnichsen, Gordon William	20
Greengrass, Charles P.	10	Standerwick, Ian Peter	28
Hall, David John Nowell	7	Starr, Abraham	13
Howard, Ian Richard	15	Strachan, Peter	4
Jorgensen, Graham Morris	8	Teehu Makimare	9
Jury, Stephen	19	Viney, Trevor Allan	22
Kaleak, Joseph	18	Walsh, Elaine	23
Kalms, Dulcie	18	Williams, John	4
Knight, Frederick John	8		

INDEX TO POLICE MEDALS

Martin, Wayne Alexander   34

INDEX TO SILVER MEDALS

Bell, Thomas William	89	McQueen, Nicholas A.W.	46
Belshaw, Sarah Jane Esther	49	Mildon, Leslie John	52
Benfield, Mark David	52	Miliakere Rarogo Vesikalou	43
Berriff, Paul	51	Milner, Peter Frank Morrell	37
Besley, David	41	Paley, Clifford W.	48
Bishop, Elizabeth	46	Pancras, Eddy	37
Blackburn, Leonard John	43	Parsons, John Valentine	43
Bonnett, Nigel Leonard	40	Pese, Meleane	40
Britten, Brian	42	Porter, Kenneth James	42
Buckfield, Donald R.J.	46	Pritchard, Margaret	47
Chrystal, Ian	39	Ranabaca, Ivamere	40
Cochrane, Raymond	55	Robertson, Keith	55
Fakalelu, Viliami Malolo	41	Rusiate Rarawa Volavola	43
Farrant, Roger Duncan	45	Saunders, Norman Douglas	52
Gibson, Thomas A.E.	42	Sayer, Robert William	38
Giles, Michael Kenneth	52	Sloane, Christopher	55
Golding, Victor Leonard	48	Somiah, Samuel Bulleh	37
Hussey, John Louis David	39	Stevenson, Peter John	50
Koso, Mathew	39	Thorne, Bryan John	52
Lawton, Frederick Arthur	49	Ward, William (clasp)	68
Lewanavanua, Marika Ului	38	Williams, Joseph Samuel	37
MacFarlane, Alexander	37		
McKechnie, Anthony M.D.L.	44		

INDEX TO BRONZE MEDALS WITH CLASPS

Name	Page
Adams, William	67
Alder, William N.	67
Allistone, John	67
Andrews, W.D.	68
Bamber, Walter Leigh	68
Barrett, Richard	68
Barry, Michael	68
Beadle, Robert Graham	68
Bear, Thomas Walter	69
Bell, Richard R.G	69
Beresford, Lord C.W.D.	69
Berry, Ernest Reginald	69
Beveridge, Alexander	69
Blackmore, M.H.	70
Blake, Stephen	70
Bolt, John	70
Bone, John J.	70
Booth, Arthur C.	70
Bowen, Henry	71
Bradley, William	71
Brinkworth, George	71
Bromley, Arthur	71
Brookes, G.C.	71
Brown, William T.	72
Brunnen, James	72
Bryce (Brice), John V.	72
Buchan, A. G.	72
Bull, John	72
Burke, Henry F.	73
Butters, Rev Wm. M.	73
Byrne, Henry	73
Campbell, Duncan	73
Carpendale, T. M.	73
Carr, John James	74
Carruthers, John T.	74
Cavill, Frederick	74
Ceil(e)y, George R.	74
Channer, George K.	75
Channon, Samuel	75
Churchill, William	75
Clowes, Alfred	75
Coleman, Albert E.	75
Congdon, George T.	76
Cook, David E.	76
Cosh, Henry	76
Craig, George	76
Craner, Edward	77
Crichton, James	77
Cruttenden, Frank P.	77
Curtis, Thomas E.	77
Dacres, Seymour H.P.	78
Davis, Frederick J.	78
Davis, Snowden	78
Donohue, Daniel	78
Douglas, Henry	78
Drake, Rev. H.M.	79
Drane, Robert	79
Dryden, James	79
Dulon, Martin	79
Dunbar, Herman	80
Edwards, Albert	80
Ellard, Joseph	80
Enderstein, Seigfred M.	80
Falconer, Joseph	80
Fant, John	81
Ferguson, W.	81
Fieldhouse, Walter	81
Finnis, James W.	81
Fippin(g), Ernest	81
Fisher, William Blake	82
Fitch, Walter	82
Flemyng, A.E.F.	82
Foot(e), Thomas	82
Foster, George	82
Freeland, Alfred	83
Fullick, Edward	83
Gladding, George	83
Glasson, Thomas S.	83
Goldsmith, Henry	83
Gonsalves, Manoel	84
Gornall, Henry	84
Grace, Edward	84
Grant, Richard S.	84
Gray, H.C.B.	84
Gregory, Thomas R.	85
Griffiths, Thomas	85
Grunsell, W.H.	85
Hammet, James L.	85
Hellyer, Edwin A.	85
Henderson, Arnott	86
Herd, Robert	86
Hodgson, Joseph R.	86
Hollingsworth, E.	86
Holloway, Graham C.	87

Name	Page	Name	Page
Holt, Hugh W.L.	87	Oakes, W.E.	97
Hood, James Samuel	87	Oliver, William M.	97
Hooton, James W.	87	Panchen, Charles	98
Hugill, Henry J.	87	Paton, Thomas	98
Humphries, Charles	88	Peebles, George	98
Hunt, Hubert H.	88	Pengelly, Ernest	98
Huntingford, W.	88	Petty, George	98
Hurcum, Charles	88	Phelps, Frederick	99
Isaacs, Henry J.	88	Philpin, Richard	99
Jappy, James	89	Pigg, Joseph	99
Jermyn, John	89	Pocklington, A.J.	99
Johns, John	89	Poë, Edmund Samuel	99
Jubb, Benjamin B.	89	Potter, James	100
Jutelet, J.G.	89	Prescott, John	100
Kemsley, H.H.	90	Prinsep, J.F.M.	100
Lamport, Frederick W.	90	Pritchard, Robert	100
Langdale, Frederick L.	90	Puttock, Robert	100
Langdon, F.G.C.	90	Quigley, Patrick	101
Langton, George	91	Quince, J.	101
Lawrey, George	91	Renforth, Stephen	101
Leonard, Peter	91	Rix, James	101
Lipscombe, Alfred	91	Robe, John	101
Little, George	91	Roberts, Ben	102
Litton, James J.	92	Robertson, R.	102
Long, Frederick	92	Ross, A.D.	102
Lovering, Richard	92	Rowland, Alexander	102
Luccock, Thomas	92	Sailing, L.	102
Mallon, Michael	92	Sandilands, Hon. F.R.	103
Martin, Robert W.	92	Sayce, Henry	103
Martins, Robert	93	Sayer, Henry	103
M(a)cAdam, F.R.P.	93	Scaife, Henry Neale	104
McAlister, William	93	Setter, Frederick W.	104
McGhee, W.	93	Setter, James H.	104
McLeod, Donald	94	Shapter, Joseph	104
McLeod, Malcolm	94	Shooter, Frank	105
McVay, M.	94	Slaughter, Frank	105
Moat, William	94	Smith, Charles Henry	105
Monger, Harold G.R.	95	Smith, Henry G.	106
Montgomery, Donald	95	Smith, Richard	106
Moss, Josiah W.	95	Spinner, Charles	106
Neilson, Isaac	95	Stark, Frederick	106
Neno, John	95	Startin, James	106
Neville, Richard John	96	Streader, William T.	107
Newsham, John	96	Sullivan, Timothy John	107
Newton, Hilary E.	96	Swan, Stewart F.	107
Noble, Andrew	96	Taylor, Joseph G.	107
Noel, Montague W.	96	Touhey, William	107
North, Richard	97	Trafford, William L.	108
O'Connor, Patrick	97	Tremayne, George	108
O'Sullivan, Charles	97	Turner, Henry C.	108

Vaughan, John Owen	108	West, Daniel	110
Vaughan-Jones, Hubert	108	Whyte, Charles	111
Vingoe, Alfred	109	Williams, James	111
Wackerell, George W.	109	Woods, Henry Byron	111
Waters, Michael	109	Wray, George H.	111
Watkins, Milson	109	Wright, Walter John	111
Watson, John	110	Young, Charles E.	112
Watts, Henry	110	Young, Henry L.	112
Wenlock, Walter B.	110		

INDEX TO ADDITIONAL BRONZE MEDALS

Allen, Charles W.P.	100		Gurton, N.E.	81
Anderson, Alfred	93		Hadley, James A.	76
Andrew, Richard Henry	4		Harris, R.G.	109
Andrews, Henry	106		Hewitt, John	75
Andrews, J.	102		Jeffery, E.C.	85
Atkinson, R.O.	108		Jerram, Lieut.	89
Ballantyne, S. McD.	104		Jones, Thomas	69
Bennett, A.N.	104		Judge, Michael J.	48
Benjamin	3		Kelsey, D.R.	106
Blackett, Henry T.	94		King George.	102
Blaylock, D.R.	95		Lancaster, J.	90
Bourke, Herbert E.M.	86		Langdale, F.L.	90
Bradley, John	91		Langdon, F.G.	90
Brazier, Edward Henry	77		Metcalfe, Roy D.	73
Bridge, G.	102		Miller, T.	94
Brown, J.	94		Martin, W.T.	95
Brown, P.	102		Owen, M.	94
Bundy, Herbert F.	86		Parkin, F.H.	95
Burns, John	91		Patry, John D.	68
Burrows, W.	90		Pratley, Henry J.	98
Byng, A.H.	87		Pentland, R.C.	84
Cape, W.R.	104		Richards, Richard A.	69
Carpenter, A.F.B.	86		Richardson, L.	71
Chan, Shu-fai	46		Scott, James W.	86
Coblenz, Stewart I.	48		Selwood, F.G.	104
Cooke, Ernest Charles	77		Sherris, Thomas Charles	38
Cosh, Henry	76		Sisley, William	98
Cotton, J.H.	90		Slimme, George	78
Crabb, Joseph	87		Sowden, Samuel D.	43
Craig, James	76		Wade, Kepple	75
Date, Steven Francis	29		Wangara, Samanu	3
Erskine, J.S.	96		Ward, George	104
George, King	111		Welch, James	71
Giddings, Albert	82			
Grieves, William	91			

INDEX TO RHS TESTIMONIALS AND PECUNIARY AWARDS

Name	Page	Name	Page
Allistone, John	67	McGregor, John	70
Anderson, W.	80	McMillan, John	97
Apakuki Ratukoka	44	Murphy, Eugene	104
Bald, Lieut.	71	Nemesio Boila	43
Ballard, Vanessa	50	Nicol, Kenneth	12
Barnham, Paul John	50	O'Neil, Janey Heap	51
Bauld, James	45	O'Neil, Steve Heap	51
Beck, Gary	55	Pearce, Nigel	54
Bleasdale, R.	75	Peni Nawadvadua	44
Buchan G.	72	Phillips, Robert John	54
Campion, Constable	83	Renforth, P.	79
Casserly, Michael John	45	Rice, A.S.	97
Coatsworth, H.	79	Ripley, Percy	104
Cooper, Roger Ian	55	Royal Berkshire Fire Service	53
Courage, Lieut.	71	Salanieta Dedevu	43
Dempsey, Daniel	95	Sando, Arthur Francis	55
Elesi Marama	44	Savirio Veimoko Boila	43
Everiss, Frederick Ian	53	Scott, Craig Robert	55
Farrell, John David	45	Scott, Olga	44
Gardiner, W.	82	Scott, L.S.	44
Giles, Elizabeth	40	Searle, James	85
Hancock, Arthur James	54	Sievey, W.T.	67
Harbor, Lawrence Alwyn	45	Sparks, David Stephen	50
Hardy, James	85	Taka Bower	44
Harvey, Thomas W.	88	Tarditi, Paul	104
Hastings, Dean Bryan	54	Tindal, Stephen Mark	55
Hawkes, S.A.	84	Upton, John	106
Hencher, Mark Richard	53	Vailea, Asppeli	41
Hulse, John	106	Vincent, Howard David	54
Jonacani Ratutini	43	Walker, O.B.	71
Jones, Philip Stanley	51	Walton J.H.	76
Jones, Simon Maurice Cooper	47	Watts, Jane	50
Kick, Brenda Joy	50	West, Gary	52
Kinloch, A.	80	Wesgate, S.W.	88
Kinloch, W.	80	Williams, Angela	50
Leech, Christopher Martin	55	Williams, Sioned	47
Loma Takape	44	Woodhead, Pennie	50
MacDonald, Peter John	54		
MacLeod, Ian Ross	51		

INDEX TO COMMONWEALTH AND OTHER AWARDS

Aspeslet, Malcom Rodney	Crown & Canada	13
Bailey, Vanessa	Canada	29
Boughton, Ian Maurice	New South Wales	27
Broekmeulen, John Christopher	Australasia	12
Busch, Ronald Peter	New South Wales	17
Calnan, David	Canada	30
Campbell, Barry John	New South Wales	9
Cuffe, Brian Leonard	Crown	42
Davey, Randy Sherman	Crown & Canada	15
Day, Anthony Shane	Australasia	28
Easton, Jack Milne	Royal Life Saving Society	11
Fader, Douglas	Crown & Canada	26
Garner, David Michael	Liverpool	20
Gleeson, Terry Haydon	Australasia	14
Howard, Ian Richard	New South Wales	17
Howard, Martin Ross	Liverpool	15
Jorgensen, Graham Morris	Australasia	8
Jury, Stephen	Australasia	19
Kaleak, Joseph	Canada	18
Kalms, Dulcie	New South Wales	18
Knight, Frederick John	New South Wales	8
Lane, Sydney James	Crown	42
Ledden, Aaron John	New South Wales	26
McCabe, John Patrick	Crown	42
McNab, John	Liverpool	17
McPherson, Bruce Walter	New South Wales	16
O'Loughlin, Frank	New South Wales	17
Peters, Rodney Stephen	New South Wales	24
Porter, Gregory Robert	New South Wales	26
Smith, Beryl Ellen	Australasia	25
Smith, James George	Liverpool	21
Smith, Peter William	New South Wales	26
Sonnichsen, Gordon William	Crown & Canada	20
Teehu Makimare	New Zealand	9
Robson, Graham Thomas	Australasia	14
Ryan, Robert John	New Zealand	11
Starr, Abraham	Crown & Canada	13
Viney, Trevor Allan	Australasia	22
Walsh, Elaine	Liverpool	23

www.ingramcontent.com/pod-product-compliance
Lightning Source LLC
Chambersburg PA
CBHW080404170426
43193CB00016B/2808